Advanced Business Chinese

高级商务汉语

下册

By Linda M Li and George X Zhang

Cypress Book Co. UK Ltd.

Chinese in Steps Series
Advanced Business Chinese Vol.II
By Linda M Li and George X Zhang

Cover Design: Wenqing Zhang

First published in Great Britain Dec 2007
Reprinted in March 2015

Cypress Book Co. UK Ltd.
Unit 6 Provident Industrial Estate
Pump Lane, Hayes
London UB3 3NE
United Kingdom
Tel: +44(0)2088382491
Fax: +44(0)2085611062

Find us at www.cypressbooks.com

Text copyright©2007 by Linda M Li and George X Zhang
Illustration copyright©2007 by Wenqing Zhang
The moral rights of the authors and illustrator have been asserted.

All rights reserved. No part of this publication may be reproduced or transmitted by any means, electronic, mechanical, photocopying or otherwise, without the prior permission of the publisher.

ISBN 978-1-84570-021-8

Printed in China

前言 - Preface

Advanced Business Chinese is designed for those who have already acquired a good command of the Chinese language but would like to gain an insight into the Chinese business practices and at the same time continue to improve their Chinese proficiency.

Advanced Business Chinese is a constituent part of the **Chinese in Steps** textbook series, and is an alternative follow-up to **Chinese in Steps V** if learners, especially those studying for business degrees, wish to focus on the business and cultural context of present day China. This book is also suitable for those with a comparable level of Chinese (a minimum of 1200 characters and 4000 words) who share an interest in Chinese business. **Advanced Business Chinese** is pitched at lower advanced level.

Advanced Business Chinese is the result of the authors' many years of experience in teaching Chinese at a number of business schools. It differs significantly from many other Advanced Business Chinese textbooks in a number of respects. It aims to meet the needs of present and future business leaders by providing a strong but practical cultural foundation to approach Chinese business issues effectively. Rather than offering more business terminology, it focuses on Chinese cultural and social traditions, such as the influence of Confucius and Sunzi that underline many aspects of business practice in China today. It presents the information from a perspective familiar to Western business managers so that both the methodology and the contents are easily accessible. Finally it incorporates some contemporary case studies on Chinese businesses so that users of the textbook can update their practical knowledge of contemporary Chinese business practice.

Advanced Business Chinese follows the same principles as the **Chinese in Steps** series in seeking balanced development of the relevant language skills. Each volume has ten lessons, and each lesson consists of a dialogue and a text; the latter, selected from various sources, is a natural follow-up to the dialogue. Exercises for each lesson reinforce students' understanding of the lesson, and additional readings combine humour with information on intellectual changes relevant to business context. All this makes **Advanced Business Chinese** unique among similar textbooks. In terms of the general content, **Advanced Business Chinese I** provides a general introduction to the social and economic background of Chinese business, while **Advanced Business Chinese II** looks into both the cultural traditions and the contemporary practice of Chinese business.

The authors would like to thank the European Business School London for its generous support, both financial and administrative, in the compilation of **Advanced Business Chinese**. The authors would also like to thank colleagues and especially students at the European Business School London for their support in piloting **Advanced Business Chinese** and for providing useful feedback. We thank China.com. for its kind permission to use some of its materials and photo images. Thanks also go to Don Starr who has taken painstaking efforts to proof-read the two volumes and offered practical advice and suggestions. Finally, we would like to express our gratitude to Xia Zhansheng, Xu Xian and Wenqing Zhang of Cypress Books Ltd for their professional dedication and help in the publication of the series. We hope you, as users of the book, will find it both beneficial and enjoyable, and we welcome your comments and feedbacks.

目 录

第十一课	儒家思想与企业管理	6
第十二课	老子思想与人力资源开发和管理	16
第十三课	孙子兵法与企业战略	26
第十四课	怎样和中国人做生意—商务习俗	36
第十五课	怎样在中国做生意-人际沟通	46
第十六课	怎样在中国做生意—跨国公司失败案例	56
第十七课	怎样在中国做生意—跨国企业成功案例	66
第十八课	介绍一个中国企业—海尔公司简介	76
第十九课	参加博览会—中国义乌国际小商品博览会	86
第二十课	全球化与中国经济之前景	96
附录一	孔子及儒家思想	106
附录二	老子及道家思想	107
附录三	孙子及《孙子兵法》	108
附录四	练习答案	109
附录五	课文英译	117
附录六	词汇表	127

第十一课　　儒家思想与企业管理

玛　　丽：李老师，我注意到中国与西方国家有很多不同之处。我在中国的时候，中国同学的用功及谦虚常让我深受感动。在中国做生意是不是跟在西方有很大的不同？

李老师：是的，每个民族都有自己的文化，而这种文化会渗透到生活的各个领域，影响着人们的思维和行动。由于不了解当地文化而导致商业失败的例子比比皆是。

大　　卫：是不是我们都要经过所谓的文化震荡？

李老师：如果你们现在多了解一些中国文化，震荡就会小一些。

大　　卫：中国文化丰富多彩，我们怎么样去了解这个多彩的文化呢？

李老师：几千年来，中华民族创造了光辉灿烂的文化，而儒家思想是中国传统文化的主干，对中华民族的文化心理、风俗习惯、道德伦理等影响极其深远。

玛　　丽：儒家思想就是我们前面所讲的儒教吧？

李老师：对。由于孔子是儒家思想的创始人，所以也称为孔子思想。现在很多人都在研究儒家文化对企业管理的影响。我们都知道，管理者和被管理者都生活在一定的文化氛围之中，文化深刻地影响着管理的原则和方法。

玛　　丽：我听说儒家文化对东亚企业影响很大。日本的企业就是在吸收了儒家文化的基础之上，创造出了一种新的企业管理模式，引起了全世界企业界的关注。

大　　卫：现代管理理论强调重视人，认为人是企业的灵魂，提倡以人为本的管理理念和策略。儒家在这方面有什么见解？

李老师：以人为本是儒家文化的基本精神，不过它偏重于人际关系协调，注重个体对群体的责任、奉献和服务，带有鲜明的群体和谐特点。

玛　　丽：我将来想去企业做管理工作，了解儒家思想对我来说很重要。李老师，您给我们介绍一下儒家思想与企业管理吧？

李老师：好。

课文　儒家思想与企业管理

孔子是儒家思想的创始人。他创造了一套完整的儒家学说，其主要思想反映在《论语》一书中。儒家思想可以供企业管理借鉴的东西很多。

"仁"是孔子思想的核心。"仁"也就是爱人。在孔子提倡的"仁"的思想中有一句名言，"己所不欲，勿施于人"。这句话被很多商人视为经营管理的黄金法则。儒家还有两个基本精神，一是"以人为本"，二是"以和为贵"。"和"就是人与人的团结合作。人与人之间，企业与企业之间经常会出现矛盾和冲突，儒家认为凡事应该"以和为贵"，"和"才是解决矛盾、持续发展的准则。孔子十分强调人和人心在国家治理中的作用，提出了"得道多助，失道寡助"、"天时不如地利，地利不如人和"的精辟论述。

孔子主张用"中庸"的方法去观察和处理自然和社会。中庸思想长期以来一直是中国人为人处事的主导原则。"中庸"就是恰到好处地掌握分寸和火候，在对立的两极之间保持某种平衡。在管理上讲究度，既不死守原则，也不随意乱变没有原则。很多人认为中国人没有原则，几乎每件事都采取个案处理的方式，但是中国人实际上有原则，这就是中庸之道。

目前，有人把世界上的管理模式划分为三种——西方、日本及中国的管理模式。西方的管理模式注重规章制度、管理组织结构等，人情味相对少些；日本式管理关注一致性，重视团队精神、忠诚与合作等；而中国式管理则强调个人与整体在企业管理中的融合与统一，在重视制度化和理性化的同时，又强调共同的价值观、和谐的人际关系以及卓越的团队精神。可以说中国式的企业管理是以法为框架，以理为中心，以情来提升的。

不同的企业管理模式可以互相借鉴，取长补短。随着全球经济一体化的发展，东西方管理文化出现了趋同倾向。未来的管理会更加强调人的价值、更具有包容性。

生词

谦虚	名/形	qiānxū	modesty; modest
渗透	动	shèntòu	permeate
思维	名	sīwéi	way of thought
导致	动	dǎozhì	lead to
比比皆是	形	bǐbǐjiēshì	abundant; everywhere
所谓	形	suǒwèi	so-called
震荡	动/名	zhèndàng	shock
光辉灿烂	形	guānghuīcànlàn	splendid, brilliant
主干	名	zhǔgàn	trunk, mainstay
道德伦理	名	dàodélúnlǐ	ethics and morality
氛围	名	fēnwéi	atmosphere
灵魂	名	línghún	soul
理念	名	lǐniàn	concept; belief
见解	名	jiànjiě	view, understanding
偏重于	动	piānzhòngyú	lay emphasis on, stress
协调	名/动	xiétiáo	harmonization; co-ordinate
奉献	名/动	fèngxiàn	contribution; devote to
和谐	名/形	héxié	harmony, harmonious
仁	名	rén	benevolence
以人为本	动	yǐrénwéiběn	regard human beings as the basis
以和为贵	动	yǐhéwéiguì	regard harmony as the most important thing
精辟	形	jīngpì	brilliant; penetrating
主张	名/动	zhǔzhāng	advocate, proposal
凡事	名	fánshì	everything
观察	名/动	guānchá	observe; observation
为人处事	名	wéirénchǔshì	dealings with others
恰到好处	形/副	qiàdàohǎochù	just right, perfect
分寸	名	fēncùn	appropriate degree
火候	名	huǒhou	timing

讲究	动	jiǎngjiu	be particular about
中庸之道	名	Zhōngyōngzhidào	Doctrine of the Mean (Confucian text)
规章	名	guīzhāng	regulation, rule
一致性	名	yízhìxìng	consistency
忠诚	名	zhōngchéng	loyalty
融合	名	rónghé	integrate, integration
卓越	形	zhuóyuè	outstanding
框架	名	kuàngjià	framework
借鉴	动	jièjiàn	draw on the experience of
取长补短	动	qǔchángbǔduǎn	learn from others strengths to make up ones own deficiencies
一体化	名	yìtǐhuà	unification, integration
趋同倾向	名	qūtóngqǐngxiàng	tendency towards convergence
包容性	名	bāoróngxìng	tolerance

专有名词

孔子 kǒngzǐ– Confucius (literally means "Master Kong") 孔子 was believed to have been born on September 28th 551 BC and died in 479 BC in Qufu, Shandong Province. He was a famous Chinese philosopher and teacher whose teachings and philosophy have deeply influenced East Asian life and thought.

论语 lúnyǔ– *Analects* It is also referred to as ***The Analects of Confucius***, a collection of sayings of Confucius allegedly gathered by his students and passed down generation after generation. It is believed to be written at the end of Spring and Autumn and the beginning of Warring States.

春秋战国 chūnqiūzhànguó– the periods of Spring and Autumn (770 BC – 476 BC) and Warring States (475 BC– 221 BC), a time in Chinese history when many schools of thought developed.

注释

1. 己所不欲，勿施于人：Do not do to others what you don't want to be done to you.

2. 得道多助，失道寡助：A just course attracts abundant support while an unjust course would find little support.

3. 天时不如地利，地利不如人和：Opportunities vouchsafed by Heaven are less important than terrestrial advantages, which in turn are less important than the unity among people.

4. 让我深受感动：让 is a causative verb, meaning "enable someone to do something" and 受感动 is in the sense of "being moved".
   例句： 1) 我生病的时候，他天天来照顾我，让我深受感动。
   2) 他十年以来一直坚持学习汉语，让人深受感动。

5. 引起……的关注：attract someone's attention
   例句： 1) 这件事并没有引起政治家的关注。
   2) 石油价格不断上涨，引起了全世界的关注。

6. 比比皆是：abundant, everywhere
   例句： 1) 在上海会说英语的人比比皆是。
   2) 在美国的超市里，中国商品比比皆是。

7. 凡事：everything 凡是：all
   例句： 1) 他很好强，凡事都要争当第一。
   2) 凡是注册的正式会员，都可以享受优惠。

练习

一、根据课文判断正误

1. 由于不了解当地文化而导致商业失败的例子不多。
2. 儒家思想是中国传统文化的主干。
3. 文化深刻地影响着管理的原则和方法。
4. 儒家文化对日本企业没有什么影响。
5. 现代文化管理理论提倡以人为本的管理理念和策略。
6. 儒家文化强调个人的利益。
7. 孔子是儒家思想的创始人。
8. "得道多助，失道寡助"是说你路子多，朋友就多。
9. "以和为贵"就是以争取团结合作为最高目的。
10. 中庸思想长期以来一直是中国人为人处事的主导原则。
11. "中庸"就是没有原则。
12. 西方的管理模式人情味相对少些。
13. 日本的管理模式和西方的差不多。
14. 中国的管理模式强调礼和情。
15. 东西方管理文化越来越不同。

二、知识问答

1. 孔子叫什么名字？他是什么地方人？

2. 以下哪一项有关《论语》的说明是不正确的？
   A.《论语》是孔子的言行录。
   B.《论语》记载了孔子论述"仁"的思想。
   C.《论语》是孔子亲自写下的经典之作。

3. 以下哪一项有关儒家的说明是不正确的？
   A. 孔子是儒家的创始人。

B. 儒家的中心思想是清静无为。

C. 孔子是伟大的思想家、政治家和教育家。

三、根据词义连线

管理文化　　　　　　越来越相似、相近

管理模式　　　　　　对不同文化感到震惊

管理理念　　　　　　管理的方式

管理策略　　　　　　管理的计谋

文化心理　　　　　　用来指导实施的方针

文化震荡　　　　　　受文化影响的思维和观念

主导原则　　　　　　对管理的看法和观点

趋同倾向　　　　　　管理实践和理论的综合表现

四、根据词语搭配连线

取长　　　　合作

光辉　　　　好处

丰富　　　　补短

恰到　　　　灿烂

为人　　　　借鉴

互相　　　　处事

死守　　　　多彩

团结　　　　原则

五、用下列词语造句

1. 主张
2. 凡事
3. 引起……的关注
4. 比比皆是
5. 取长补短

六、选词填空

1. （国界、发行、模式、先后、文化、研究、引起、其次）

　　从第一次世界大战到现在，世界上____出现了四次孔子研究热潮。孔子被列为世界十大____名人，《论语》的____量居世界十大名著的第二位。儒学的生命力已经远远超过中国的____。近年来，世界经济理论____的一个热点就是对"东亚发展模式"的研究。第二次世界大战后，首先是日本，____是"四小龙"以及近几年中国经济的高速增长，____世界极大的关注。东亚工业区向世界展示了一种非西方经济的发展____。

2. （请教、品德、取得、获得、任用、侮辱、使唤、实施）

　　子张向孔子____什么是仁。孔子说："能在天下____五种品德就可以说是仁了。"子张说："请问是哪五种____呢？"孔子说："谦恭、宽厚、诚信、勤敏、慈惠"。谦恭就不会受到____，宽厚就能____群众，诚信就会得到别人的____，勤敏就会____工作成效，慈惠就能够____别人。"

七、讨论题

1. 当代企业管理文化中最能体现儒家思想的理念是什么？

2. 如果你是经理，你会不会用儒家思想去管理你的企业？

阅读思考

团结的力量

从前，有一个老汉，他有20个儿子。他这20个儿子个个都很有本领，可是他们都认为自己本领最高，不把别人放在眼里。老汉见到儿子们这种互不相容的情况，非常担心。他常常苦口婆心地教导儿子们要相互团结友爱，可是儿子们对父亲的话都是左耳朵进、右耳朵出，根本没放在心上。

老汉一天天老了，他明白自己在世的日子不会很久了。一天，他把儿子们召集到病床前，对他们说："你们每个人都放一根筷子在地上。"儿子们照办了。老汉让儿子把地上的一根筷子折断。小儿子稍一用力，筷子就断了。老汉又说："现在把剩下的19根筷子捆在一起，再试着折断。"儿子们个个使出了吃奶的力气，可是都没能将筷子折断。

老汉语重心长地开口说道："你们都看得很明白，一根筷子很容易折断，可是合在一起的时候就折不断了。你们兄弟也是如此，如果单独行动，很容易遭到失败，可是如果20个人联合起来，就会产生出无比巨大的力量，这就是团结的力量啊！"

儿子们终于领悟了父亲的良苦用心，都流着泪说："父亲，我们明白了，您就放心吧！我们一定互相帮助，团结友爱。"

思考：折筷子的故事告诉了我们什么道理？

生词

本领	名	běnlǐng	skill, ability
互不相容	动	hùbùxiāngróng	unable to tolerate each other
苦口婆心	副	kǔkǒupóxīn	urge time and again with good intention
语重心长	形/副	yǔzhòngxīncháng	sincere (ly) and honest (ly)

幽默

哲学家和船夫

一个哲学家与一个船夫之间正在进行一场对话。

"你懂哲学吗?"

"不懂。"

"那你至少失去了一半的生命。"

"你懂数学吗?"

"不懂。"

"那你失去了百分之八十的生命。"

突然一个巨浪把船打翻了,哲学家和船夫都掉到了水里。看着哲学家在水中挣扎,船夫问他:"你会游泳吗?""不……会……""那你就失去了百分之百的生命。"

第十二课　　老子思想与人力资源开发和管理

玛　　丽：李老师，我对您讲的中庸之道很感兴趣。在中国的时候，我发现中国人说话、做事总是给自己留有后路，这是不是受了中庸之道的影响？

李老师：我想是吧。中庸之道已经深深扎根于中国的文化之中，中国人会下意识地这么去做。

大　　卫：中国的改革开放是渐进式的，这也是受了中庸之道的影响吧？

李老师：你说得对，我认为中国经济改革的成功得益于中庸之道。你们知道俄罗斯也进行了改革，可是俄罗斯的改革比较激进，实行了全面私有化。

玛　　丽：两国改革的结果相差很大，中国的经济快速增长，俄国的经济则一度出现了负增长。

大　　卫：对，可是中庸之道会不会给企业管理带来困难？

玛　　丽：是啊，会不会出现赏罚不够分明、企业上下人人追求"以和为贵"的局面呢？

李老师：这就要看企业的高层领导怎么样了。企业文化是企业的高层领导造就的。所以高层领导的任命非常重要。

大　　卫：儒家在这方面有什么独特的见解？

李老师：儒家思想强调企业领导人的自身修养，以身作则。而道家思想对企业的高层领导任命及人力资源开发很有借鉴作用。

玛　　丽：道家是不是我们前面提到的道教？

李老师：不完全是。道教是宗教，它是在道家学说的基础上建立起来的。道家学说源于春秋战国时期，是老子创建的。

大　　卫：我只听说过孔子，从来没听说过老子。

李老师：老子是中国古代一位伟大的思想家，其主要思想集中反映在《道德经》一书中。

玛　　丽：李老师，人力资源管理是我们管理课程中的主要内容。我很想知道老子思想在这方面能为我们提供什么样的帮助。

李老师：人力资源管理与开发直接影响着一个企业的竞争能力，所以非常重要。现在我们一起来看看老子在这方面的论述。

课文　老子思想与人力资源开发和管理

老子姓李，叫李耳，大约生活于公元前571至471年之间，著有《老子》，又称《道德经》。后人称《道德经》是领导术、管理术。老子的学说对当今企业的人力资源开发和管理具有指导意义。

根据老子的观点，人力资源管理的前提是要了解人，只有了解一个人，才能明智地去用他。但是怎样去了解一个人呢？怎样去看待一个人的能力与价值呢？老子认为，用人者首先得明智，要有"自知之明"，不持有偏见、不听信谗言、不嫉妒贤才、不贪公受贿……只有这样的人，才能使真正优秀的人才得到重用。

在关于什么是人才的问题上，老子认为世上无废人。也就是说，一个好的领导者，要善于发现每个雇员的长处，用其所长，避其所短，使其为企业谋利益。领导者用人不可以追求十全十美，因为世界上没有十全十美的人。世界上也没有不可用之人，只有还没有被发现的人才和不会用人的人。在识别优秀人才上，老子认为，领导者要善于透过现象看本质，不被事物的表面现象所迷惑。如果光看表面、忽视本质、忽视潜力，就会埋没真正优秀的人才。领导者还应该明白，善于卖弄的人未必有真才实学，因此应该提拔那些埋头苦干的员工。

识别人才的目的在于用好人才，因此如何恰当地发挥人才的潜力非常重要。老子认为领导者应该善于放权。最好的领导者，因为善于调动属下的积极性，常常使人感觉不到他的存在。当属下把工作任务完成时，所有的人都认为"这是我自己干的"。当然，领导者要善于集权，这主要表现为在重大的决策问题上当机立断。在决策的执行过程中，领导者没有必要频频过问，要给属下施展才能的机会，要充分调动属下的工作积极性。

领导者对下属要指令明确。我们知道事物都是运动的，但事物在一定时间和空间里又是相对静止的。在老子思想里，"变"是一个十分重要的概念，但老子又强调说领导者不可以经常改变指令，使属下无所适从。领导者应该"以不变应万变"，使属下在事物的变动中有所遵循，达到既定的目标。

生词

人力资源	名	rénlìzīyuán	human resources
扎根于	动	zhāgēnyú	be rooted in
下意识	副	xiàyìshi	subconsciously
得益于	动	déyìyú	benefit from
赏罚分明	动	shǎngfáfēnmíng	be fair in rewards and punishment
造就	动	zàojiù	achieve; train
任命	名/动	rènmìng	appointment; appoint
独特	形	dútè	distinctive, unique
自身修养	名	zìshēnxiūyǎng	personal self improvement
以身作则	动	yǐshēnzuòzé	set an example oneself
前提	名	qiántí	premise, prerequisite
明智	形	míngzhì	sensible, wise
自知之明	名	zìzhīzhīmíng	wisdom that comes from self knowledge
谗言	名	chányán	slander, malicious talk
嫉妒	动/名	jídù	envy, be jealous of
贤才	名	xiáncái	virtuous and talented people
贪公受贿	动	tāngōngshòuhuì	greedy and corrupt
废人	名	fèirén	useless people
雇员	名	gùyuán	employee
十全十美	形	shíquánshíměi	perfect
现象	名	xiànxiàng	(external) appearance; phenomenon
本质	名	běnzhì	(basic) nature
迷惑	动/名	míhuò	mislead; confusion
埋没	动	máimò	neglect; bury
卖弄	动	màinong	show-off
未必	副	wèibì	not necessarily
真才实学	名	zhēncáishíxué	real ability and learning
提拔	动/名	tíbá	promote
埋头苦干	动	máitóukǔgàn	devote oneself to work, work hard
属下	名	shǔxià	subordinate

积极性	名	jījíxìng	initiative; enthusiasm
当机立断	动	dāngjīlìduàn	be decisive, make immediate decision
频频	副	pínpín	frequently
施展	动	shīzhǎn	demonstrate, utilize
指令	动/名	zhǐlìng	give instruction
静止	形	jìngzhǐ	static
概念	名	gàiniàn	concept
无所适从	动	wúsuǒshìcóng	be at a loss as to what to do
遵循	动	zūnxún	comply with; follow
既定	形	jìdìng	predetermined

专有名词

老子 – Lao Zi or Lao Tzu, Lao Tse, Laotze

老子 is a major figure in Chinese philosophy who lived in the 5th century BC. He is credited with writing the *Dao De Jing* and is recognized as the founder of Taoism. Little is known about his life. Tradition says he was born in Ku Prefecture (苦县) in the state of Chǔ (楚), which today is Lùyì County (鹿邑) in Henan province.

《道德经》– Dao De Jing or Tao Te Ching

It is said that the book was originally written by 老子. The book contains about 5000 characters, and its main theme is the Dao (Way), which can be interpreted as referring to Nature, or how the natural world functions. It is also believed that the **Dao De Jing** was written as a guideline for emperors on how they should rule the empire in a more natural way "Ruling by not ruling". This can be found in the numerous references in the **Dao De Jing** which state: "Not exalting men of worth prevents the people from competing" and "Not putting high value on rare goods prevents people from being bandits" and "Human hunger is the result of over taxation. For this reason, there is hunger."

注释

1. **领导术，管理术**：the art of leadership, the art of management

2. **使其为企业谋利益**：使 is a causative verb like 让 in meaning, and 谋 means "seek, plan for". So the sentence means "to enable them to work for the benefit of the enterprise".

3. **用其所长，避其所短**：use a person's strengths and avoid their weaknesses

4. **以不变应万变**：be unchanging in ones response to the constant changes

5. **善于**：be good at
   例句：1）他很善于交际。
   2）做自己喜欢和善于做的事，上帝也会助你走向成功。

6. **十全十美**：perfect
   例句：1）在他眼里，他的女朋友十全十美。
   2）世界上并没有十全十美的政治或经济制度。

7. **忽视**：ignore, neglect
   例句：1）环境保护不容忽视。
   2）由于父母的忽视，孩子的音乐天才差点被埋没了。

8. **遵循**：follow, comply with, observe
   例句：1）西部生态环境建设必须遵循自然规律和经济规律。
   2）教育收费应该遵循什么样的原则？

9. **未必**：not necessarily
   例句：1）闪光的未必都是金子。All that glisters is not gold.
   2）惩罚未必是提高出勤率的好方法。

练习

一、根据课文判断正误

1. 大部分中国人办事都给自己留后路。
2. 中国经济改革的成功和中庸之道伦理没有关系。
3. 俄罗斯在经济上实施全面私有化。
4. 《道德经》是儒家的重要著作。
5. 道教是在道学的思想上建立起来的。
6. 道家思想可以运用到现代企业的人力资源管理中。
7. 老子是中国古代一位伟大的思想家。
8. 老子认为用人者不必什么都会，可是要有自知之明。
9. 老子认为世界上有些人根本没有用。
10. 领导者要善于发挥每个人的特长。
11. 领导者应该提拔那些埋头苦干的员工。
12. 善于卖弄的人不一定有真才实学。
13. 为了调动属下的积极性，领导者要频频过问属下的工作情况。
14. 如果属下感觉不到领导者的存在，那说明他不是一个好领导。
15. 领导者不可以经常改变指令。

二、知识问答

举例说明

1. 什么是"自知之明"？

2. 什么是"以不变应万变"？

3. "世上无废人"是什么意思？

三、根据词义连线

听信谗言　　　　　　　　留有回旋的余地
埋没人才　　　　　　　　很会炫耀、显示自己
领导术　　　　　　　　　相信别人说某人的坏话
留有后路　　　　　　　　不重视有才华的人
用其所长　　　　　　　　没有重视以后能够发挥的能力
贪公受贿　　　　　　　　当老板的艺术
忽视潜力　　　　　　　　贪污公家的财产、接收他人给的钱财
善于卖弄　　　　　　　　使用他擅长的技能

四．根据词语搭配连线

无所　　　　　　　　　　立断
真才　　　　　　　　　　苦干
埋头　　　　　　　　　　实学
自知　　　　　　　　　　适从
当机　　　　　　　　　　之明
以身　　　　　　　　　　才能
赏罚　　　　　　　　　　作则
施展　　　　　　　　　　分明

五、用下列词语造句

1. 善于
2. 十全十美
3. 忽视
4. 遵循
5. 未必

六、选词填空

1.（容器、柔弱、精神、完全、张开、为、胜、遇到、滴水、即将）

老子的师父常纵_____离开人世。老子问师父："老师！你还有最后的教示吗？" 常纵回答说："你看牙齿和舌头，哪个刚强？哪个_____？" 老子说："牙齿刚强！舌头柔弱。" 常纵缓缓_____嘴巴："你看！我的嘴里还有什么？" 原来常纵的牙齿已经_____掉光了，嘴巴一张开，只有柔弱的舌头还在。常枞说："这就是我为你上的最后一课，柔弱_____刚强。"老子含着眼泪说："今后，我将以谁为师？" 常枞说："你应该以水_____师。" 水最柔软，放入圆形的_____之中就成为圆形，放入方形的容器之中则成为方形。 "水"最柔弱，水_____阻碍物就会转个弯，但是流向并没有改变。水看起来软弱无力，却含有无尽的内力，俗话说："_____可以穿石"，又说："抽刀断水水更流"。"智者如水"，我们都应当学习"水"的_____。

2.（问、储存、挡住、原来、脚掌、软软、那么、背、为什么、忍耐）

动物园里的小骆驼_____妈妈："妈妈，为什么我们的睫毛_____长？"骆驼妈妈说："长长的睫毛可以_____风沙，使我们在风暴中看得到方向。" 小骆驼又问："妈妈，为什么我们的_____那么驼，丑死了！"骆驼妈妈说："这个叫驼峰，可以帮我们_____大量的水和养分，使我们能在沙漠里不吃不喝_____十几天。"小骆驼又问："妈妈，为什么我们的_____那么厚？" 骆驼妈妈说："那能让我们重重的身体不陷在_____的沙子里啊。"小骆驼高兴坏了："_____我们这么有用啊！可是妈妈，_____我们还在动物园里，不去沙漠远足呢？"

七、讨论题

1. 老子的用人之道和当代西方人力资源管理有何异同之处？
2. 你最欣赏老子用人思想的哪一点？

阅读思考

求千里马

传说古代有一个非常喜爱骏马的国王，为了得到一匹千里马，许诺一千两黄金。可是天下的千里马很少，派去买马的人找了三年，连千里马的影子也没有见到。

一个官员看到国王闷闷不乐，便自告奋勇地对国王说："您把买马的任务交给我吧！我一定会买到千里马的。"国君听了非常高兴，马上答应了他的请求。这个官员东奔西跑，用了3个月时间，总算打听到了千里马的踪迹。可是当他见到那匹马时，马已经死了。

虽然这是一件令人非常遗憾的事，但是这位官员并不灰心。马虽然死了，但它却能证明千里马是存在的。既然世上的确有千里马，就用不着担心找不到第二匹、第三匹，甚至更多的千里马。想到这里，他马上用500两金子买下了那匹死马的头，兴冲冲地带着马头回去面见国王。国王见到死马头愤怒地说道："我要的是活马，而你却花重金买了一个死马头。你拿死马的头献给我，你到底想干什么？！"那位官员不慌不忙地说："请国王不要生气，听我慢慢解

释。世上的千里马数量稀少，我花了3个月时间，好不容易才遇见一匹这样的马。我用重金买下死马的头，仅仅是为了抓住一次难得的机会，向大家证明千里马真的存在，同时向天下人表明国王购买千里马的诚意和决心。如果这一消息传开，即使有千里马藏匿于深山密林、海角天涯，养马人听到了君王是真心买马，必定会主动来献马。"

果然不出所料，此后不到一年的时间，接连有好几个人牵着千里马来拜见国君。

思考： 诚意和耐心在成功中的重要性

生词

骏马	名	jùnmǎ	fine horse
许诺	名/动	xǔnuò	promise
闷闷不乐	形	mènmènbúlè	despondent
自告奋勇	动	zìgàofènyǒng	volunteer (to do something)
东奔西跑	动	dōngbēnxīpǎo	run hither and thither
总算	副	zǒngsuàn	finally, eventually
踪迹	名	zōngjì	trace
遗憾	形/名	yíhàn	regret, be a pity
甚至	副	shènzhì	even
兴冲冲	副	xìngchōngchōng	in high spirits
愤怒	名/形	fènnù	anger; angry
重金	名	zhòngjīn	a substantial amount of money
诚意	名	chéngyì	sincerity
不慌不忙	形/副	bùhuāngbùmáng	unflustered, calmly
藏匿于	动	cángnìyú	concealed in
海角天涯	名	hǎijiǎotiānyá	the ends of the earth
不出所料	副	bùchūsuǒliào	as expected
牵	动	qiān	lead, pull

幽默

特 长

老板杰克到警察局报案:"有个流氓冒充我的推销员,在镇上赚了10万英镑!这比我所有的雇员在客户身上赚到的钱还要多。你们一定要找到他!"

警察说:"我们会抓住他,把他关进监狱的!"

"关起来干什么?我要聘用他!"老板杰克说。

第十三课　　孙子兵法与企业战略

大　卫：从前面两课我们了解到，不论是儒家还是道家，他们都强调人的价值，都强调和谐相处。以人为本已经深深扎根于中华民族的文化之中。

玛　丽：我在中国的时候，还听人说起孙子和《孙子兵法》这本书。据说古今中外的军事家都使用他的理论来指导战争，而且他的基本理论和思想还被运用到了现代企业决策和管理方面。

李老师：你说得对。《孙子兵法》已经被译成29种文字，在世界上广为流传。

大　卫：孙子又是谁？

李老师：孙子名字叫孙武，是中国著名的军事家。他生于2500年前的春秋末年。他写的《孙子兵法》是中国著名的兵书。

大　卫：这部古老的军事著作，对当代商务运作有什么作用呢？

李老师：军事与企业管理虽然是不同的领域，但它们确实有许多相似之处。市场就是战场，做生意就像打仗一样，大家都想取胜。

玛　丽：中国人常说："三十六计，走为上计。"三十六计是不是《孙子兵法》中的计谋？

李老师：《三十六计》是中国古代著名的兵书之一，其各种计谋都可以在《孙子兵法》中找到理论根据。

大　卫：李老师，《孙子兵法》的主要思想是什么？

李老师："知己知彼，百战不殆"是贯穿于全书始终的思想，至今仍被认为是科学真理。

玛　丽：您能不能给我们举个例子，看看它是怎么在商业中应用的？

李老师：行。孙子讲在作战指挥中要"避实击虚"，那我就讲个有关的小故事吧。这个故事叫"田忌赛马"，讲的是田忌在孙膑的帮助下运用"知己知彼，以己之长，攻人之短"和"丢卒保车"的混合计谋取得赛马胜利的经过。这在经济学上又叫"错位竞争"，就是用自己的优势去和别人竞争，后发制人。

课文　　田忌赛马

齐国的大将田忌很喜欢赛马，有一回他和齐威王进行比赛。他们把各自的马分成上、中、下三等。由于齐威王每个等级的马都比田忌的马强得多，所以比赛了几次，田忌都失败了。

田忌觉得很扫兴，比赛还没有结束就要离开赛马场。这时，他的好朋友孙膑招呼他过去。孙膑拍着他的肩膀说："我刚才看了赛马，威王的马比你的马快不了多少呀。"还没等孙膑说完，田忌瞪了他一眼说："想不到你也来挖苦我！"孙膑说："我不是挖苦你，我是说你再同他赛一次，我有办法准能让你赢了他。"田忌疑惑地看着孙膑："你是说另换一匹马来？"孙膑摇摇头说："一匹马也不需要更换。"田忌毫无信心地说："那还不是照样得输！"孙膑胸有成竹地说："你就按照我的安排办吧。"

齐威王屡战屡胜，正在得意洋洋地夸耀自己马匹的时候，看见田忌和孙膑走来，便站起来说："怎么，你还不服气吗？"田忌说："当然不服气，咱们再赛一次！"说着，"哗啦"一声，把一大堆银钱倒在桌子上，作为他下的赌注。齐威王一看，马上让随从把前几次赢得的银钱全部抬来，另外又加了一千两黄金，也放在桌子上。齐威王说："那就开始吧！"

比赛开始了。孙膑先以下等马对齐威王的上等马，第一局输了。齐威王站起来说："想不到赫赫有名的孙膑先生，竟然想出这样拙劣的对策。"孙膑不去理他。接着进行第二场比赛。孙膑拿上等马对齐威王的中等马，胜了一局。齐威王有点心慌意乱了。第三局比赛，孙膑拿中等马对齐威王的下等马，又战胜了一局。这下，齐威王目瞪口呆了。比赛的结果是三局两胜，当然是田忌赢了齐威王。还是同样的马匹，由于调换了比赛的出场顺序，就得到了转败为胜的结果。

生词

军事家	名	jūnshìjiā	military strategist
计谋	名	jìmóu	stratagem
贯穿于	动	guànchuānyú	run through, permeate
始终	副	shǐzhōng	from beginning to end, always
指挥	动/名	zhǐhuī	command
丢卒保车	动	diūzúbǎojū	lose a soldier to save the chariot, sacrifice a minor thing to save the major one
错位竞争	动	cuòwèijìngzhēng	skewed competition
后发制人	动	hòufāzhìrén	win through counter-attacking strategy
避实击虚	动	bìshíjīxū	avoid the strong and attack the weak
扫兴	名/动	sǎoxìng	feel dejected
挖苦	动/名	wākǔ	mock, ridicule
疑惑	副/动	yíhuò	doubtfully, be doubtful
胸有成竹	副/形	xiōngyǒuchéngzhú	knowingly; confident in ones plans
屡……屡……	副	lǚ…lǚ…	repeatedly
得意洋洋	形/副	déyìyángyáng	conceited
夸耀	动	kuāyào	brag about, show off
服气	动	fúqì	admit defeat, concede
赌注	名	dǔzhù	(gambling) stake
随从	名	suícóng	entourage
赫赫有名	形	hèhèyǒumíng	illustrious, very famous
竟然	副	jìngrán	unexpectedly
拙劣	形/副	zhuōliè	poor, inferior
心慌意乱	形	xīnhuāngyìluàn	agitated
目瞪口呆	形	mùdèngkǒudāi	dumbstruck, stupefied
顺序	名	shùnxù	order
转败为胜	动	zhuǎnbàiwéishèng	turn defeat into victory

专有名词

孙子 Sūnzi – Sunzi, Suntzu, also known as 孙武

He was born around 535 BC in present day Shandong Province, China, but the date of his death is unclear. He is an acclaimed military strategist and the author of *Art of War*, a most influential work in Chinese military history.

《孙子兵法》 Sūnzi bīngfǎ – *Art of War*

It is an acclaimed Chinese military strategy masterpiece said to have been composed by Sunzi. Much of the spirit of the work has been absorbed into the Chinese life and culture.

孙膑 Sūnbìn – Sun Bin

Born about a century after Sunzi, Sun Bin is a descendent of Sunzi and also a military strategist who knew the art of war very well. He is claimed to be the author of *Sunbin's Art of War* (《孙膑兵法》), another important text on the subject. Unfortunately, much of his writing is now lost.

齐威王 Qíwēiwáng -- King Wei of the state of Qí (齐)

Qi state is in present day Shandong Province, and one of the seven major powers during the Warring Period (475 BC - 221 BC).

田忌 Tíanjì – Tianji

A general of the state of Qi who was first attracted by Sun Bin's strategies and won many battles with the help of Sun's military advice.

注释

1. 知己知彼，百战不殆 (zhī jǐ zhī bǐ, bǎi zhàn bù dài): If you know your enemy as well as yourself, you will not be defeated in a hundred battles.

2. 三十六计，走为上计: Of the thirty six stratagems, the best option is to flee.

3. 以己之长，攻人之短 (yǐ yǐ zhī cháng, gōng rén zhī duǎn): Use one's strong points to attack another's weak points.

4. 就……而论: as far as …is concerned
   例句： 1）就销售量而论，那两家公司差不多。
   2）就速度而论，没有人比得上老于。

5. 准: for sure (colloquial)
   例句： 1）看这天气明天准下雨。
   2）听你的口气你准是没有到过中国。

6. 胸有成竹: confident (in ones plans)
   例句： 1）如果做好了充分的准备，你就会有胸有成竹的感觉。
   2）只有胸有成竹，才能应对自如。

7. 屡……屡……: again…again; time after time
   例句： 1）考试不能作弊，可是他屡教屡犯。
   2）他不是个谈判高手，公司派他去谈判他屡谈屡败。

练习

一、根据课文判断正误

1. 儒家和道家都强调和谐相处。
2. 《孙子兵法》已经被译成多种文字。
3. 孙子名字叫孙膑。
4. 孙子的军事理论对经商有指导意义。
5. 市场和战场非常相似。
6. 三十六计，走为上计。
7. "错位竞争"是不该和别人竞争，可是偏要竞争。
8. 齐王的马每一等都比田忌同等的马好。
9. 由孙膑出对策的比赛第一局田忌赢了。
10. 第二局比赛齐王赢了。
11. 第三局比赛田忌赢了。
12. 齐王输了是因为他的马出了毛病。
13. 田忌赢了是因为他在马出场的顺序上作了调整。
14. 田忌使用了丢卒保车的计谋。
15. 田忌赛马说明了计谋的重要性。

二、知识问答

1. 举例说明战场与商场都有哪些相同之处？
2. 举例说明什么是丢卒保车？
3. 孙子和孙膑是什么关系？

三、根据词义连线

拙劣　　　　　　　　　　差不多一样的地方

避实击虚　　　　　　　　躲开厉害的，打击软弱的

毫无信心　　　　　　　　打三场赢了两场

后发制人　　　　　　　　既了解自己也了解对手

三局两胜　　　　　　　　颠倒位置和对手比高低

知己知彼　　　　　　　　一点儿信心也没有

错位竞争　　　　　　　　非常粗恶、非常笨

相似之处　　　　　　　　等对方先动手，然后自己再反攻

四、根据词语搭配连线

心慌　　　　　　　　　　口呆

目瞪　　　　　　　　　　意乱

赫赫　　　　　　　　　　为胜

运用　　　　　　　　　　洋洋

转败　　　　　　　　　　计谋

古今　　　　　　　　　　流传

广为　　　　　　　　　　中外

得意　　　　　　　　　　有名

五、用下列词语造句

1. 贯穿于
2. 准
3. 屡……屡……
4. 胸有成竹
5. 就……而论

六、选词填空

1. 他_____着我的肩膀对我说："我一定支持你！"　　　　（打/拍）

2. 我认为要想赢就得_____大赌注。　　　　　　　　　　（下/上）

3. 张老师是我的导师，我的论文就是他_____的。　　　　（指导/指示）

4. 在印度，_____表示同意。　　　　　　　　　　　　　（点头/摇头）

5. 小王生气了，一天都没有_____我。　　　　　　　　　（喜欢/理）

6. 你少_____我，谁都知道我的汉语不怎么样。　　　　　（挖苦/痛苦）

7. 汉字是一种_____的文字。　　　　　　　　　　　　　（悠久/古老）

8. 虽然他的汉语很好，可是他对同声翻译_____信心。　　（充满/毫无）

9. 就是你读了博士也_____找不到工作。　　　　　　　　（照样/照常）

10. 你有政策，我有_____。　　　　　　　　　　　　　 （对策/决策）

11. （分别、作为、只好、等待、早晚、傻瓜、限制、交纳、想出、注视）

美国对进口的货物_____得十分严格。凡是进口高级手套，必须_____重税。面对这一严厉措施，一个进口商_____了一条妙计，他把从国外购买的一万双高级皮手套按左、右手_____包装，先把一万只左手套运回了国。海关要进口商交纳重税，他却说，这一万只手套不能_____"手套"来使用，因此收重税不合理。海关人员_____收了一般货物的进口税。但是，海关人员也不是一群_____，他们预料那一万只右手套_____也会到来，因此密切_____进入海关的货物。不久，另外一万只右手套运至海关，海关人员马上做好了准备，_____进口商来提货。

七、讨论题

1. 田忌为什么会赢？

2. 丢卒保车对卒是不是不公平？

阅读思考

新田忌赛马

齐王赛马输了，心中很不高兴。为此齐王想出了一条妙计。齐王派人把田忌找来，对田忌说："上次赛马你赢了，三天后我再和你赛一次。"田忌吃了一惊，田忌赛马的规则只能用一次，再用就不灵了。齐王又说："这次赛马你先出马，我后应马。你赢了，我的好马都给你，你输了，我杀你全家。"田忌想这次他是死定了，这时孙膑却托人带来口信，"有我在，保你全家无事。"

三天的限期到了，人们都想看看田忌还有什么高招赢齐王。田忌的第一匹马拉上场了。人们看到，这匹马根本不是战马，它梳了无数个小辫子，更可笑的是还化了妆。

比赛开始了，齐王的宝马飞腾着奔向前方，不多时就把田忌的白马抛在后面。田忌的白马似乎不在乎输赢，慢慢悠悠地扭着屁股走着。齐王高兴极了，而田忌几乎要昏了过去。

就在这个时候，形势发生了逆转。只听田忌的马嘶叫了一声，齐王的宝马急忙回转身来，朝着田忌的马跑了过去。田忌的白马向齐王的宝马抛了一个媚眼儿，齐王的宝马扑通一声跪倒在白马的面前。再后来，田忌的大白马遛溜达达地朝目标走去，齐王的宝马跟在身后随同前往。

齐王真是气坏了，没想到田忌用母马勾引公马，使公马乖乖成了母马的感情俘虏。还用比吗？以后几场一定还是母马战胜公马。

此计乃36计中的美人计。

思考：这一计怎么样？有没有更好的计？

生词

妙计	名	miàojì	cunning plan
限期	名	xiànqī	deadline
化妆	名/动	huàzhuāng	make up (with cosmetics)
飞腾	名/动	fēiténg	fly along
抛	动	pāo	leave behind; throw
扭	动	niǔ	twist, wiggle
屁股	名	pìgu	buttocks
昏	动	hūn	pass out, faint
逆转	名/动	nìzhuǎn	unexpected turn (of events)
嘶	动	sī	neigh
媚眼	名	mèiyǎn	coquettish look
扑通	象声	pūtōng	fall with a flop
跪	动	guì	kneel down
溜溜达达	副	liúliudáda	saunter
勾引	动/名	gōuyǐn	seduce
俘虏	名	fúlǔ	captive

幽默

买效率

老板为了提高效率，给工厂买了一台机器人。一个月后，机器人公司的代表访问工厂，却发现机器人连包装都没有拆开。他迷惑地问："工厂为什么买机器人？"

老板回答："为了提高效率。"

"那为什么不安装？"

"我对工人说，如果谁偷懒，我就用机器人换他，所以工人都很努力，效率提高了两倍。"

第十四课　　怎样和中国人做生意—商务习俗

大　　卫：李老师，听说中国有不少规矩，很多商人都是因为不懂得这些规矩而失败的。

李老师：是的。每个国家都有自己的规矩，中国的这些规矩基本上都是儒家文化的体现。欧美商人和亚洲商人相比，不得不更多地顾及与中国文化上的差别。

玛　　丽：中国的"送礼"文化也是西方人不容易掌握的。我在中国的时候不是被认为小气、就是被认为无知。

李老师：中国是一个注重礼仪和回报的国家，送礼就成了人际交往中的一个重要环节。出门做客、求人帮忙，总免不了要带一些礼物给主人，以表示客人的诚意。

大　　卫：中国人都喜欢送什么东西？

李老师：礼物的选择需要考虑到送礼的对象。去朋友家不需要准备什么太贵重的礼物，买些水果、点心就可以了。礼物的包装也不必太讲究。

玛　　丽：现在的年轻人也喜欢送花、送酒、送巧克力。另外，他们也很喜欢西方小工艺品。

李老师：玛丽，你发现了没有，中国人在接受礼物后不会马上打开包装，而是放在一边，等客人走了以后才打开。

玛　　丽：没错，他们这种做法真给我留了面子。说实在的，我送的礼物总是包装最漂亮、价格最便宜。

大　　卫：我听说去中国朋友家吃饭，主人总是说："没什么好菜，凑合着吃。"

李老师：几千年来，中国人把儒家的谦虚作为最高尚的美德之一，很多现有的习俗也都是从这一观念派生出来的。贬低自己意味着对别人的尊重。

玛　　丽：李老师，和中国人做生意，我们应该注意些什么呢？

李老师：知己知彼，入乡随俗。和中国人做生意，要尽量多熟悉中国的商务习俗。

课文　　商务习俗

中国人在与人交往时注重对方的头衔和社会地位。一般情况下都用职位来称呼，如"赵经理"、"李厂长"、"谢总"等。这样表示你对他的尊敬。对于退休后的官员，人们还是恭恭敬敬地叫他的头衔，这是因为中国人不忘前情。"老师"现在不仅仅用来称呼教书的人，也可以用来称呼那些年龄、资历、学问都比较高的人。

去中国前不仅应阅读一些介绍客户的资料，而且要阅读一些有关中国概况的资料，最好学几句汉语。用汉语打招呼能给主人留下良好的印象，说明你尊重、欣赏他说的语言。递名片的时候要用双手，接到名片时要先看一会儿再放入口袋。中国人喜欢红色，不喜欢黑色和白色，因此在服饰、礼品包装上要多加注意。礼品不要太贵重，那有行贿的嫌疑，但是也不能太便宜，那样表示你不太重视主人。最好送些价格适中、具有西方特色的工艺品。中文的"钟"与"终"同音，因此不要给中国人送钟，另外也不要送利器和雨伞。中国人的吉利数字是六和八，四是最不吉利的数字。

谈话的话题也很重要。一次商务会谈能否获得成功，有赖于主人在同你进餐时对你的了解。餐桌上避免谈论台湾、西藏、法轮功和人权等问题。因为在这些问题上中西方的看法分歧很大。吃饭的时候中国人喜欢劝酒，喜欢为客人夹菜。中国人喜欢细细地品尝美食，因此有"叭哒"嘴的习惯，喝汤时也往往"吱吱"作响，这在西方人看来难以接受。不过西方人的一些习惯，中国人也难以接受，比如大声擤鼻涕、咂手指、咬指甲等。回请中国人的时候先要弄清楚他们是否喜欢吃西餐、是否有睡午觉的习惯。一般来说，大部分的人都喜欢吃中餐，并且有睡午觉的习惯。

不过中国正在发生变化，越来越国际化了。

中国人尊重长者，喜欢帮助别人。如果对你过分照顾，那是因为他们尊重你。中国人说话婉转，喜欢用"也许"、"可能"等字眼，这是因为他们爱面子，不想直接拒绝你，那么你也要给他们留面子。谈判时出言不要太重，尊重对方，不妄加评判。如果你使主人或客人感到难堪，即使是一时疏忽，也往往会给业务带来严重损失。

生词

规矩	名	guīju	rules and regulations
顾及	动	gùjí	take into account, consider
礼仪	名	lǐyí	ritual
环节	名	huánjié	link
凑合	动	còuhe	make do, put up with
高尚	形	gāoshàng	revered
派生	动	pàishēng	derive
贬低	动	biǎndī	debase, belittle
入乡随俗	动	rùxiāngsuísú	follow local customs
恭恭敬敬	副	gōnggōngjìngjìng	respectfully
头衔	名	tóuxián	title (of a person)
欣赏	动	xīnshǎng	appreciate, show appreciation for
服饰	名	fúshì	clothing
嫌疑	名/动	xiányí	suspicion, suspect
利器	名	lìqì	sharp object, weapon
法轮功	名	Fǎlúngōng	Falungong
夹菜	动	jiācài	pick up food with chopsticks
叭哒	象声	bādā	smack lips, sound made when eating
擤鼻涕	动	xǐngbítì	blow one's nose
咂	动	zā	lick, suck
咬	动	yǎo	bite, chew
午觉	名	wǔjiào	afternoon nap

相让	动	xiāngràng	offer to others
婉转	形	wǎnzhuǎn	indirect
妄加评判	动	wàngjiāpíngpàn	make unwarranted criticism
难堪	形	nánkān	embarrassed
疏忽	动	shūhū	neglect, overlook
一时疏忽	名	yìshíshūhū	a single oversight, a careless moment

注释

1. **不是……就是……**：if not X, then must Y

    例句： 1）这里只有我们两个人，不是你去，就是我去。
    2）我明年要去公司实习，不是去银行，就是去保险公司。

2. **把……当作**：take.. as…

    例句： 1）不少电脑公司都把微软当作竞争的对手。
    2）我要把学好中文当作头等大事来看待。

3. **有赖于**：dcpcnd on

    例句： 1）和平的国际环境有赖于各国共同的努力。
    2）产品的销售有赖于良好的销售渠道。

4. **难以**：difficult to

    例句： 1）他给的条件太好了，我难以拒绝。
    2）不少西方人都说中国人难以捉摸。

5. **免不了**：difficult to avoid

    例句： 1）喜欢读书的人免不了经常去逛书店。
    2）常在河边走免不了会湿鞋。

6. **吃独食**：to eat on one's own without offering to others. This is considered to be very self-centred and unsociable in Chinese society.

练习

一、根据课文判断正误

1. 欧美商人和亚洲商人相比，更能适应中国文化。
2. 中国人非常重视送礼。
3. 中国人送礼都是为了求人办事。
4. 中国人收到礼物后一般不马上打开包装。
5. 到朋友家做客不用带礼物。
6. 中国人不十分重视礼品包装。
7. 在中国，谦虚是最高尚的美德之一。
8. 在中国，"老师"可以用来称呼职业不是老师的人。
9. 中国人喜欢数字"四"和"八"。
10. 中国人爱面子，所以吃饭没有声音。
11. 西方人喜欢大声擤鼻涕、咂手指。
12. 中国人不送"伞"作为礼物，因为它不够珍贵。
13. 很多中国人认为西藏和台湾应该独立。
14. 你最好别在午饭后给中国朋友打电话。
15. 中国人说话婉转是给对方留面子。

二、解释下列图表

2007春节送礼调查

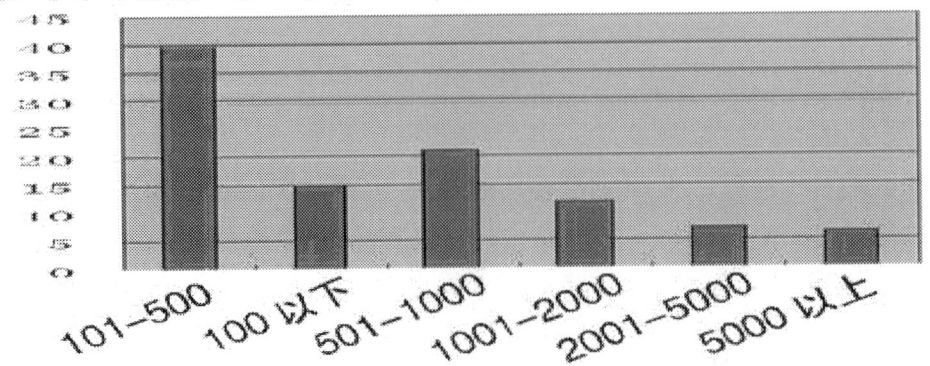

希望收到什么礼物？

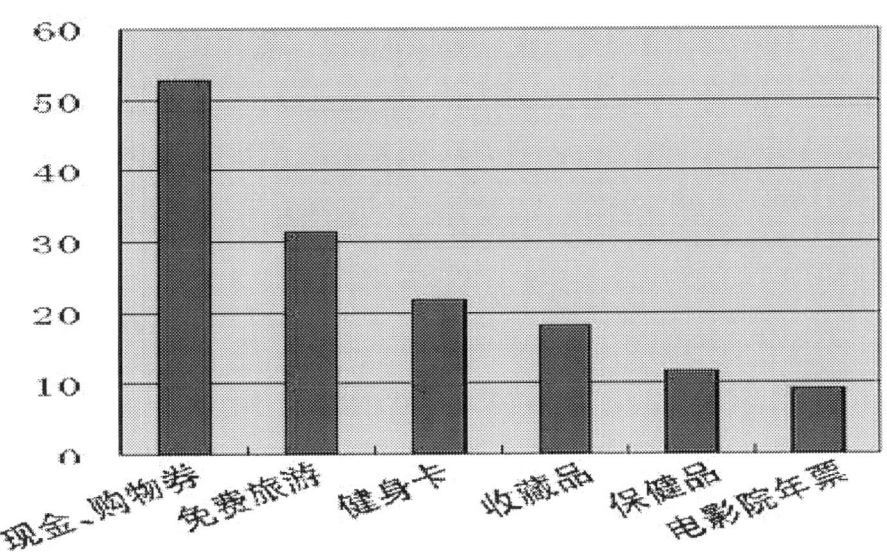

您准备送给谁礼物？

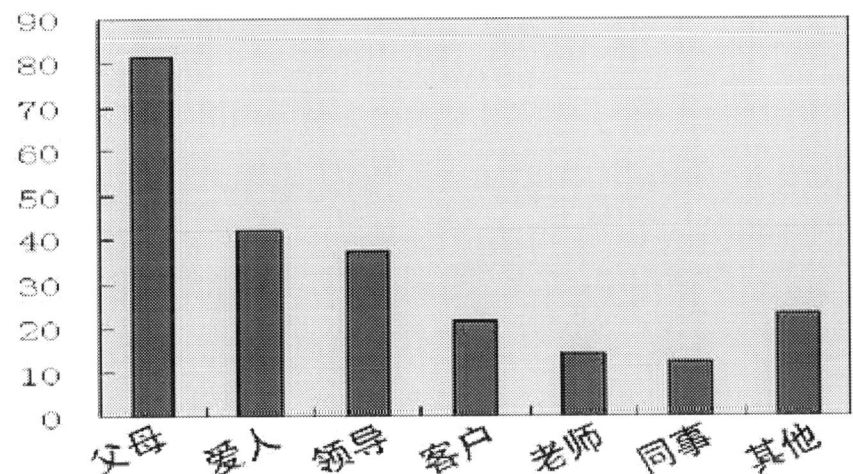

三、根据词义连线

商务习俗　　　　　　　　　到一个地方要遵循这个地方的风俗
入乡随俗　　　　　　　　　价格不高不低，正合适
过分照顾　　　　　　　　　不指出其错误或弱点
留面子　　　　　　　　　　做生意的风俗习惯
难堪　　　　　　　　　　　以前的情义一直记在心中
不忘前情　　　　　　　　　照料得太周全了
价格适中　　　　　　　　　非常没面子
一时疏忽　　　　　　　　　偶尔不小心出错了

四、根据词语搭配连线（可以有多种搭配）

顾及　　　　　　　　　　　颜色
贬低　　　　　　　　　　　食物
产生　　　　　　　　　　　客人
呷　　　　　　　　　　　　诚意
表示　　　　　　　　　　　分歧
回请　　　　　　　　　　　手指
吉利　　　　　　　　　　　他人
品尝　　　　　　　　　　　对方

五、用下列词语造句

1. 有赖于
2. 把……当作
3. 不是……就是
4. 免不了
5. 难以

六、选词填空

1. 员工一定要遵守公司的_____。　　　　　　　　（规矩/规定）
2. 做生意跟交朋友一样，一定要有_____　　　　　（诚实/诚意）
3. 英国人送礼非常____包装。　　　　　　　　　　（讲究/研究）
4. 常回家看看父母就是对父母的_____。　　　　　（汇报/回报）
5. 老王今天喝醉了胡说八道，真令人_____。　　　（难看/难堪）
6. 你这样做太_____了。　　　　　　　　　　　　　（过度/过份）
7. 这是我们公司的新产品，免费_____。　　　　　（品尝/品味）
8. 公司应该努力_____人才的流失　　　　　　　　（避免/避开）
9. 新的董事长将在他们三人中_____。　　　　　　（派生/产生）
10. 我们不应该_____他的诚意。　　　　　　　　　（怀疑/疑问）

11．（毫无、意识到、期限、竞争、派去、可是、动静、废物）

　　日子一天天过去了，_____进口商就是不出现。眼看超过了保管_____，进口商还是毫无_____。海关人员沉不住气了，他们认为进口商可能是_____了什么，情愿放弃那批货。于是他们只好将那一万只"无人认领"的右手套当作_____拍卖。 一位_____背景的小商人，在没有任何_____的情况下、以最低的价格将"废物"买走了。当然，这位小商人是进口商_____的。

七、讨论题

1. 你遇见过中国人讲面子的情况吗？

2. 西方人讲不讲面子？

阅读思考

孔融让梨

孔融有五个哥哥，一个小弟弟。孔融四岁的时候，有一天，家里吃梨。一盘梨子放在大家面前，哥哥让弟弟先拿。你猜，孔融拿了一个什么样的梨？

他不挑好的，不拣大的，只拿了一个最小的。父亲看见了，心里很高兴：别看这孩子才四岁，还真懂事，就故意问孔融："这么多的梨，又让你先拿，你为什么不拿大的，只拿一个最小的呢？"

孔融回答说："我年纪小，应该拿个最小的；大的留给哥哥吃。"父亲又问他："你还有个弟弟，弟弟不是比你还要小吗？"孔融说："我比弟弟大，我是哥哥，我应该把大的留给弟弟吃。"

你看，孔融讲得多好啊。他父亲听了，哈哈大笑："好孩子，好孩子，真是一个懂事的好孩子。"

孔融四岁，知道让梨。上让哥哥，下让弟弟。孔融这种谦虚礼让的美德，受到人们的称颂。后代教育家们又把"孔融让梨"写进启蒙课本《三字经》中，以此教育儿童学会礼貌让人。

思考：故事中的说教和西方文化传统有何异同？

第十五课　　怎样在中国做生意－人际沟通

大　卫：李老师，您说的这些对我来说太有用了。

玛　丽：我初到中国的时候，对中国人用间接的方式回答直接的问题感到大惑不解。现在我倒觉得西方人说话太直了。

大　卫：中国人那样婉转不会引起误会吗？

李老师：有这样一个故事。一个欧洲商人在上海投标。他找到了主管官员，觉得得到的答复是"令人愉快的"。他以为可以中标，结果却被拒绝了。中国人出于礼貌，没有把话说明，这个欧洲人却认为自己"受骗"了。

大　卫：这真是个不该有的误会。李老师，如果在中国跨国公司当老板的话，还应该注意些什么问题？

李老师：那你可要小心啊。领导者要以身作则。你们听说过一个关于老板穿牛仔裤上班的故事吗？

玛　丽：没有。您给我们讲讲。

李老师：有一天，一位英国老板穿了一条牛仔裤去上班。第二天，一位中国员工也穿了条牛仔裤去上班。可是老板大发雷霆。

玛　丽：那没道理。为什么他可以穿，别人就不可以穿？！

李老师：是啊，那位员工也是这样说的。可是老板说："我穿的是黑色牛仔裤，你穿的是蓝色牛仔裤。"

玛　丽：我明白了，在英国黑色代表郑重，而蓝色就没有这个功能。

李老师：可是中国员工不明白，以为是老板搞特殊化。后来费了好大的劲才平息了这场风波。

大　卫：这说明老板的工作没做好。他应该让员工明白这两种颜色的区别。明文规定什么能穿、什么不能穿。

玛　丽：我觉得他应该入乡随俗，不管是黑牛仔裤还是蓝牛仔裤都应该让穿。

李老师：跨国公司里的企业管理不容易。作为一家跨国经营的企业，应该根据所在国的国情、合作伙伴以及客户的实际情况，形成一套适用于所在国的管理模式。

大　卫：看来照搬"成熟、先进的经营管理模式"是行不通的。

生词

孔融	专名	Kǒng Róng	a descendant of Confucius and a well known man of letters in the later Han Dynasty
懂事	形	dǒngshì	sensible
称颂	名/动	chēngsòng	praise
启蒙	名/动	qǐméng	enlighten, didactic
谦虚礼让	形	qiānxūlǐràng	modest and give precedence to others
《三字经》	名	Sānzìjīng	*Three Character Classic*, a primer for children to learn reading
礼貌让人	形	lǐmàoràngrén	be polite and give precedence to others

幽默

爱称

莫里斯请好朋友巴里到自己的家里吃晚饭。巴里留意到莫里斯每次和妻子说话都要用一些很亲密的称呼，例如："宝贝儿，亲爱的"等等。

晚饭后巴里感叹地对莫里斯说："结婚都快20年了，你还像新婚那样叫她，我实在很羡慕你们。"莫里斯悄悄地说："其实我在三年前就忘了她的名字。"

课文　　怎样在中国做生意–人际沟通

由于文化不同，即使是西方先进的管理方法搬到了中国也可能行不通。跨文化管理的良方是沟通与交流。西方投资者发现，在中国，按照他们的标准来寻找合资伙伴或得力的管理人员并不是一件容易的事情。他们怀疑中方是否了解西方的商业实践，而中国人却发现他们过于武断，听不进中方人员提出的建议。

西方人在企业管理中习惯于"业务是业务，个人关系是个人关系"的理念，而中国人则认为两者可以合二为一。西方人的批评是对事不对人，中国人却往往是先对人再对事。西方人喜欢用直接的方式进行交流，在企业管理过程中如果发生了人与人之间的矛盾，他们喜欢摆出大量的事实来说明事情的真相，语言十分直白。中国人则认为这样做比较伤面子，喜欢采取比较含蓄的做法，保全当事人的面子。

中国雇员希望企业有"社会型福利"，如上下班的班车、周末娱乐等等，西方人则倾向于对工作以外的事情甩手不管，留出私人空间。西方人觉得政策不透明可能会带来麻烦，中国人却认为这不是什么大不了的问题。中国雇员习惯于大事化小、小事化了，西方管理者则希望及时知道出现的问题并尽快解决。中国人倾向诉诸权威、先例，西方人则看重管理创新。西方人喜欢看效果，中国人偏爱编织"关系"。西方雇员会直接提出加薪要求，而中国雇员却一般不会这么做。 中国人比较被动，喜欢等待别人的赏识。中国员工，特别是工程技术人员，大多属于"埋头苦干"型，希望"伯乐识才"，却不知道维护自己的权益，更缺乏现代商业谈判意识。另外中国员工特别不能容忍侮辱人格的体罚。在儒家传统文化中，父母和长者可以体罚幼者，但中国人现在已经摒弃了儒家的这一部分。特别是经过共产党多年的管理和教育，平等已经深入人心。体罚员工会毁了一个企业的名誉，导致企业破产。

简而言之，中国雇员的人格基本特征是具有较强的依附性，比较内向，追求和谐，不直接跟领导顶撞，不随意得罪任何人。但是他们的公平意识很强，表面上看起来不在乎，心里却十分在意。他们也很注重个人道德修养、注重节俭，重视家庭生活，注意身体保养，不酗酒、不熬夜，不狂欢。

生词

大惑不解	形	dàhuòbùjiě	be extremely puzzled
大发雷霆	动	dàfāléitíng	fly into a rage, lose one's temper
投标	动/名	tōubiāo	put in a bid
郑重	形/副	zhèngzhòng	serious, solemn
特殊	名/形	tèshū	special (see Note 3 for 特殊化)
照搬	动/名	zhàobān	copy, follow slavishly
实践	动/名	shíjiàn	practice
合二为一	动	hé'èrwéiyī	combine two into one
武断	形	wǔduàn	arbitrary, autocratic
含蓄	形	hánxù	indirect, implicit
倾向于	动	qīngxiàngyú	tend to
甩手不管	动	shuǎishǒubùguǎn	wash one's hand of
遇事化小	动	yùshìhuàxiǎo	minimise problems
诉诸	动	sùzhù	resort to
伯乐	专名	Bólè	name of famous horse expert (see Note 5)
体罚	名/动	tǐfá	corporal punishment
侮辱人格	动	wūrǔréngé	insult one's integrity
摒弃	动	bìngqì	discard, give up
深入人心	动	shēnrùrénxīn	reach the hearts of the people
依附性	名	yīfùxìng	anaclisis
内向	名	nèixiàng	introverted personality
顶撞	动	dǐngzhuàng	contradict, clash with
得罪	动	dézuì	offend
酗酒	动/名	xùjiǔ	drink excessively
熬夜	动	áoyè	stay up late into the night

注释

1. **即使……也……**：even if…would still
   例句：　1）即使下雨，我们也要去。
   　　　　2）即使公司目前有困难，我们也要保证公司的市场地位。

2. **招标；投标；中标**：invite public bidding; submit a bid; win the bid
   例句：　1）这次的招标工作进行得很顺利，投标的公司很多。
   　　　　2）最后中标的公司是一家知名的跨国企业。

3. **搞特殊化**：enjoy special treatment, seek special privileges
   例句：　1）领导干部应该以身作则，不搞特殊化。
   　　　　2）我不是搞特殊化，因为我晕车，所以我才坐飞机去的。

4. **导致**：lead to, cause
   例句：　1）我觉得这种做法会导致市场的混乱。
   　　　　2）外国投资者的大量涌入导致了房价上涨。

5. **伯乐识才**："伯乐" is the name of a legendary immortal looking after horses in heaven. Referred originally to Sun Yang of the Spring and Autumn Period, who found an excellent horse for the king of the state of Chu. He was later given the epithet Bole in recognition of his ability to identify good horses. The term was later used for people good at spotting talents.

练习

一、根据课文判断正误

1. 中国人喜欢用间接的方式回答直接的问题。
2. 外国人常常由此产生误会。
3. 要求员工遵守的，领导者不一定要遵守。
4. 在英国，黑色和蓝色都代表郑重。
5. 西方人认为"业务是业务，个人关系是个人关系。"
6. 中国雇员希望企业能常常组织周末娱乐活动等等。
7. 中国人喜欢摆出大量的事实来说明事情的真相。
8. 西方人不介意跟领导直接顶撞。
9. 中国雇员喜欢直接提出加薪要求。
10. 中国雇员重视家庭生活，下班一般都赶快回家。
11. 中国人爱编织"关系"。
12. 西方人不随意得罪人。
13. 中国人喜欢熬夜，喜欢狂欢。
14. 由于深受儒家文化的影响，中国员工不在乎体罚。
15. 照搬"成熟、先进的经营管理模式"是行不通的。

二、知识问答

1. 根据你的了解，列出你们国家员工的特点

2. 根据你的了解，列出下列各国员工的特点

中国	英国	美国	德国	日本

三、根据词义连线

诉诸　　　　　　　　　　你目前逗留的那个国家

大发雷霆　　　　　　　　将两者合为一个整体

得罪人　　　　　　　　　很清楚的书面规定

平息风波　　　　　　　　大发脾气，大声斥责

明文规定　　　　　　　　惹恼了他人

合二为一　　　　　　　　求助于

所在国　　　　　　　　　简单地说

简而言之　　　　　　　　把事态抑制住

四、根据词语搭配连线（可以有多种搭配）

引起　　　　　　　　　　真相

等待　　　　　　　　　　面子

摆出　　　　　　　　　　身体

保养　　　　　　　　　　事实

容忍　　　　　　　　　　机会

保全　　　　　　　　　　误会

说明　　　　　　　　　　权益

维护　　　　　　　　　　体罚

五、用下列词语造句

1. 导致
2. 照搬
3. 沟通
4. 深入人心
5. 即使……也……

六、选择填空

1. 东南亚的金融_____给泰国造成了很大的影响。　　　（风浪/风波）
2. 让中国人下跪是_____他们。　　　　　　　　　　　（侮辱/耻辱）
3. 政府_____地承诺加强知识产权保护工作。　　　　　（郑重/严重）
4. 他不会汉语，跟他沟通很_____。　　　　　　　　　（费劲/费尽）
5. 当面_____上司是要付出代价的。　　　　　　　　　（顶撞/碰撞）
6. 人人都有自己_____的颜色。　　　　　　　　　　　（偏爱/偏见）
7. 你这样做_____意义。　　　　　　　　　　　　　　（毫无/任何）
8. 我的助手不够_____。　　　　　　　　　　　　　　（得力/得当）
9. 公司的制度不_____，员工们都很有意见。　　　　　（透明/透视）
10. 我希望能和你一起来_____美好的人生。　　　　　（编织/编制）

11. （充分、于是、担任、辛苦、管辖、前任、借助、团队、治理、因为）

　　孔子的学生子贱在某地方_____官吏的时候，时常弹琴自娱，不管政事，可是他所_____的地方却民兴业旺。这使他的_____百思不得其解，_____他每天从早忙到晚，也没有把地方治理好。_____他去请教子贱："为什么你能_____得这么好？"子贱回答说："你只靠自己的力量去进行，所以十分_____；而我却是_____别人的力量来完成任务。" 其实，一个聪明的领导人，就应该像子贱那样，_____发挥属下的作用，发挥_____协作的精神。

七、讨论题

1. 你是否碰到过因文化差异而产生矛盾的情况？

2. 你会怎么着手解决由于文化冲突引起的问题？

八、成语趣解连线

最高的人	包罗万象	extremely quick
最大的手	一步登天	to seize every opportunity
最大的嘴	顶天立地	very stingy
最大的步	度日如年	to have a meteoric rise
最贵的字	一毛不拔	to hoodwink the public
最尖的针	一字千金	days wear on like years
最吝啬的人	气吞山河	upstanding and dauntless
最长的一天	一手遮天	all-inclusive
最大的容量	风驰电掣	full of daring
最快的速度	无孔不入	Very precious

小知识

汉语的惯用语

惯用语是口语中短小定型的习惯用语。例如：开夜车、唱高调、穿小鞋、走后门、泡蘑菇、半瓶醋、眼中钉、钻空子、耳边风……

惯用语活泼生动，常用来比喻一种事物或行为，相当于一个词或词组，它的意义往往不能简单地从字面上去推断。如"炮筒子"是指性情急躁或心直口快的人，"狗腿子"是指坏人的帮凶。惯用语虽然是一种较固定的词组，但定型性比成语要差些。"无孔不入"是成语，"钻空子"是惯用语。我们可以把"钻空子"拆开说成"钻了一个空子"、"钻了我们的空子"等等。但是"无孔不入"不能说成"无一孔不入"，更不能说成"无我们的孔不入"。

阅读理解

鹬蚌相争 渔人得利

战国时，秦国很强大，赵国、燕国都比较弱小，然而赵惠文王却打算出兵攻打燕国。为了避免战争，燕国的苏代跑到赵国去求见赵惠文王。苏代对惠文王讲了这样一个故事：

一只河蚌好久没上岸了。有一天出了太阳，河岸上十分暖和，于是河蚌爬到岸上，张开蚌壳晒太阳。河蚌只觉得浑身舒服极了，它懒洋洋地打起瞌睡来。这时，一只鹬鸟飞过来，用长长的尖嘴伸进蚌壳去啄河蚌的肉。河蚌猛一惊醒，迅速用力把蚌壳合上，将鹬的尖嘴紧紧地夹住了。

鹬鸟对河蚌说："我看你能在岸上呆多久！如果今天不下雨，明天不下雨，你就会被干死。"

河蚌也十分强硬地说："我看你能饿多久！我今天不松开你的嘴，明天也不松开你的嘴，你就会被饿死。"

两个小东西就这样对抗着，谁也不肯相让。这时，一位渔夫走过来，把蚌和鹬都捉住了，高兴地拿回家去了。

苏代的故事刚一讲完，赵惠文王就拍着自己的脑袋说："多谢先生的启发，如果我们小国间自相残杀，让秦国从中得利，那我们跟这故事里的鹬和蚌又有什么区别呢？"

于是，赵王取消了攻打燕国的念头。

思考：鹬蚌相争的故事说明了什么道理？在商业上有何应用价值？

生词

鹬	名	yù	snipe
蚌	名	bàng	clam
渔夫	名	yúfū	fisherman
蚌壳	名	bàngké	clam shell
浑身	名	húnshēn	whole body
懒洋洋	副	lǎnyángyang	lazily
打瞌睡	动	dǎkéshuì	doze off, have an nap
啄	动	zhuó	peck
强硬	形/副	qiángyìng	tough, unyielding
对抗	动/名	duìkàng	resist, fight
猛一惊醒	动	měngyījīngxǐng	suddenly wake up/come to realise
自相残杀	动	zìxiāngcánshá	fight among themselves and kill each other

专有名词

秦国	Qínguó	Qin, one of seven states in Warring States Period
赵国	Zhàoguó	Zhao, one of seven states in Warring States Period
燕国	Yānguó	Yan, one of seven states in Warring States Period
赵惠文王	Zhào Huìwén Wáng	King Huiwen of Zhao
苏代	Sūdài	name of a famous persuasive speaker

幽默

理发

比尔在上班时间去理发，碰巧遇见了公司经理。他想躲，可是已经来不及了。

"比尔，你竟然在上班时间来理发，这是违反公司规定的。"

"先生，我是在理发。可是我的头发是在上班时间长的呀。"

"不完全是这样，有些是在你自己的时间里长的。"

"您说得完全正确，先生，所以我并没把头发全部剃掉。"

第十六课　　怎样在中国做生意—跨国公司失败案例

大　　卫：当跨国公司老板真的不容易。

玛　　丽：不了解文化差异做什么都不容易。

李老师：如果有一个中国代表团到英国你爸爸的公司访问，你会怎么来招待他们？

大　　卫：我会安排他们参观公司、会谈和看样品。周末的时间让他们自己安排，不限制他们的自由

玛　　丽：是不是应该安排他们看看伦敦的景点？

李老师：十分有必要。中国人希望给他们安排一个比较紧凑的时间表。这是热情好客、尊重对方的表现。如果只拿出一个松散的时间表，中国人会认为你没有诚意。

大　　卫：我想我还应该请他们吃饭，吃中餐。

李老师：对。有一个美国公司与法国公司竞争失败的例子。美国人邀请中方到美国来参观了他们上乘的设备，并准备以低于竞争对手的价格出售，但是法国人最终赢得了这个项目。

玛　　丽：法国人邀请中国人吃中餐了？

李老师：对，法国人很少邀请中国人吃法国餐。他们尊重中方代表，多听少说。相比之下，中国人觉得法国人有人情味，更容易相处。

大　　卫：别人的经验教训对我们很有借鉴作用。李老师，能不能给我们介绍几个外国公司在中国成功或失败的例子？

李老师：这方面的例子还真不少。我就先给你们讲一个失败的例子吧，因为"失败乃成功之母。"

玛　　丽：老师，这句话是什么意思？

李老师：就是说成功都是建立在失败的基础之上的。一般来说，跨国公司在中国受挫主要有三种原因，一是狭隘的民族主义观念；二是套用经典经营管理模式；三是缺乏遵守东道国市场秩序和道德准则的观念。下面的案例是根据李海龙先生的文章改编的，讲的是美国一家电器公司在中国投资失败的原因。

课文　　跨国公司在中国失败案例之一

美国一家电器公司的模式化经营管理策略是：首先利用与投资国具有一定优势的企业合资来登陆，然后培植自己的市场优势。以最快速度获得合资公司的管理权，从生产、管理到销售全部由美方掌管。同时，以最快的速度建立自己的销售网络以及相关的运营系统，避开合资方的销售渠道，自建网络，使自己在技术和市场方面都占到足够的优势，不至于在今后的市场运作中被对方所制约。

这是个逻辑严密的经营管理模式，为什么在中国行不通呢？

首先，在与中国企业合资之前，公司委托了一家不十分了解中国市场的"国际广告公司"制作广告。广告力度不够，使美国名牌未得到消费者的认可。

其二，公司一开始就建立了一整套类似美国本土的管理机构。在公司不景气的情况下，对成本控制不严，仅美方四位管理人员一年的费用就达80万美元。另外，由于急于建设自己的销售网络，公司的管理成本直线上升，超过了合资企业本身的最大承受力。

其三，冰箱生产的化工原料执意从美国进口，其成本高出1/3多。另外对职工管理也失策，人心涣散，直接影响了生产。这些都导致了公司生产成本过高。而且习惯于规范的美国人不知道"三角债"是何物，结果应收款不能及时收回，造成公司资金周转不灵。

其四，公司直接从国外聘请职业经理人进入合资企业管理层。由于这些人对中国国情和市场不熟悉，只能使用在其他国家一贯的管理方法，结果出现了许多错位的管理经营策略，造成了经营失败。譬如在其合资生产微波炉的经营管理中，公司按照老规矩，把市场推进方案先传到香港分部，然后再传到美国总部去审批，一个来回拖了两三个月，等到方案批准时，市场的商机早已丢失。

由于一味克隆所谓"成熟的管理模式"，再加上本身对中国市场不熟悉，结果投入了大笔的资金，公司反而被中国同行挤出了市场。这个案例表明，虽然外来公司通过投资控股可以获得企业的主导权，但如果不能充分利用本土合资伙伴的管理经验，同样会导致企业的失败。

生词

招待	动/名	zhāodài	treat, receive
样品	名	yàngpǐn	sample product
紧凑	形	jǐncòu	busy, full (schedule)
松散	形	sōngsǎn	slack, sparse (schedule)
诚意	名	chéngyì	sincerity
上乘	名	shàngchèng	top grade, high end
受挫	名	shòucuò	suffer from setback
狭隘	形	xiá'ài	narrow
套用	动/名	tàoyòng	indiscriminately adopt
东道国	名	dōngdàoguó	host country
秩序	名	zhìxù	order, rules
登陆	动	dēnglù	to land, to get into a market
培植	动/名	péizhí	cultivate, nurture
掌管	动/名	zhǎngguǎn	take charge of, control
制约	动/名	zhìyuē	constrain
委托	动/名	wěituō	commission (somebody to do something)
认可	名	rènkě	recognition, approval
承受力	名	chéngshòulì	ability to bear
执意	动/副	zhíyì	insist on
人心涣散	动	rénxīnhuànsàn	no shared sense of belonging
三角债	名	sānjiǎozhài	debt involving three parties
聘请	动/名	pìnqǐng	recruit, recruitment
一贯	副	yíguàn	uniform, unchanging
一味	副	yíwèi	blindly, invariably
克隆	动	kèlóng	clone; copy
控股	动	kònggǔ	have controlling share
上策	名	shàngcè	best strategy

注释

1. **不至于**：be unlikely

   例句： 1）我们必须做好准备，这样才不至于被动。

   　　　2）他很有经验，不至于连这个小问题都看不出来。

2. **得到……认可**：gain the approval or acceptance of

   例句： 1）通过多年的努力，该产品终于得到了很多顾客的认可。

   　　　2）这个公司还没有得到有关部门的认可。

3. **一上来就**：from the very beginning

   例句： 1）公司一上来就遇到了财务困难。

   　　　2）他一上来就说，他不是来听我们解释的。

4. **造成**：give rise to, bring about (an unsatisfactory situation or state)

   例句： 1）他的失误给公司造成了巨大损失。

   　　　2）据说这次空难是人为错误造成的。

5. **反而**：on the contrary, instead

   例句： 1）他很不讲理，不但不认错，反而说是别人的不对。

   　　　2）公司的业务非但没有减少，反而比以前增加了。

练习

一、根据课文判断正误

1. 中国代表团希望给他们安排一个紧凑的时间表。
2. 应该安排中国代表团参观旅游景点。
3. 中国人很喜欢吃西餐,因为西方的东西都是先进的。
4. "失败乃成功之母"是说失败好比妈妈,成功好比儿子。
5. 失败有时候是由于狭隘的民族主义。
6. 不遵守东道国市场秩序和道德准则,企业也会成功的。
7. 该公司的经营管理策略是不要被合资伙伴控制。
8. 公司委托了一家中国广告公司制作广告。
9. 美国的这个电器名牌深受美国消费者的欢迎。
10. 公司的管理成本太高了,超过了合资企业本身的承受力。
11. 冰箱生产的化工原料从美国进口是因为中国的材料不能用。
12. 公司直接从中国当地聘请高级经理人员。
13. 该合资公司归香港分部管,事事要先通报分部。
14. 公司的失败是由于中国的顾客太挑剔了。
15. 公司的失败是由于套用经典经营管理模式。

二、知识问答

1. 举例说明:

1) 狭隘民族主义的具体表现是什么?

2) 合资企业的优势和缺陷。

3) 高层经理当地化的好处。

2．写出下列公司的英文名字

参考网站：www.google.com

沃尔玛	惠尔浦
星巴克	百事可乐
强生	波音
惠普	戴尔
微软	摩托罗拉
摩根士丹利	花旗集团
摩根大通	高盛集团
美国运通	美林国际
雪佛龙	福特汽车
西门子	宝马
汉莎集团	欧莱雅
家乐福	雷诺
标致	沃尔沃
爱立信	诺基亚
雀巢	瑞士信贷

三、根据词义连线

热情好客	人心不齐
人心涣散	从实践中得到的知识、技能或教悔
竞争对手	认为自己的民族又好又重要
经验教训	对客人很友好，照顾得很周全
模式化经营	不能正常调配
逻辑严密	敌手
狭隘民族主义	以固定的方式运作
周转不灵	条理性很强

四、根据词语搭配连线 （可以有多种搭配）

限制	经验
委托	控制
严格	经营
跨国	自由
丢失	商机
缺乏	报告
及时	调整
审批	制作

五、用下列词语造句

1. 不至于
2. 仅……就……
3. 反而
4. 一上来就……
5. 得到……认可

六、选词填空

1. 总统的行程安排得很_____。 （紧密/紧凑）
2. 讲演比赛的_____按汉语拼音排列。 （秩序/顺序）
3. 他_____支持英格兰足球队。 （一贯/连贯）
4. 道路_____是这里堵车的原因。 （狭隘/狭窄）
5. 这本书里有北京所有旅游_____的介绍。 （景点/景色）
6. 这是一个有关人力资源的_____案例。 （经典/法典）
7. 公司年年都送一部分管理人员出国_____。 （培植/培训）
8. 大学毕业后她_____要去非洲工作。 （执意/随意）
9. 我们公司服务周到，产品质量_____。 （上乘/上层）
10. 中国政府认为中国不能_____西方的政治模式。 （套用/套取）

11．（把握、观察、而、检讨、结果、遭遇、至于、委屈）

　　有些人失败之后会成功，_____有些人失败之后不会成功，这是什么原因呢？我们不是常说"失败乃成功之母"吗？为什么会有不同的_____呢？

　　仔细_____，你就会很容易发现，那些后来成功的人，_____失败却不怨天尤人，不乱发牢骚，反过来好好_____自己，充实自己，等待下一次机会的到来。_____那些再次失败的人，他们总是把自己的失败归罪于别人，认为自己受_____、吃大亏，因而到处发牢骚。这样的话，就算下次机会到来，他也_____不住，自然无法获得成功。

七、讨论题

1．你是否还知道其他在中国不成功的企业案例？

2．你认为怎样才能避免失败？

阅读思考

塞翁失马

从前，有位老汉住在与胡人相邻的边塞地区，人们都称他为"塞翁"。有一天，塞翁家的马不知道什么原因迷路了，回不来了。邻居们得知这一消息以后，纷纷表示惋惜。可是塞翁却不以为然，他说："丢了马当然是件坏事，但谁知道它会不会带来好的结果呢？"

果然，没过几个月，那匹迷途的老马又从塞外跑了回来，并且带回了一匹胡人骑的骏马。于是，邻居们又一齐来向塞翁贺喜，然而塞翁却说："唉，谁知道这件事会不会给我带来灾祸呢？"

塞翁的儿子非常喜欢这匹骏马，天天骑着马兜风。终于有一天，儿子从飞驰的马背上掉了下来，摔断了一条腿，造成了终生残疾。邻居们闻讯后赶紧前来慰问，可是塞翁还是那句老话："谁知道它会不会带来好的结果呢？"

又过了一年，胡人大举入侵中原，边塞身强力壮的青年都被征入伍，结果十有八九都在战场上送了命。而塞翁的儿子因为腿有残疾免服兵役，躲过了这场灾难。

这个故事后来成为一句成语："塞翁失马，焉知祸福。"它说明好事与坏事都不是绝对的，在一定的条件下，坏事可以引出好的结果，好事也可能会引出坏的结果。

思考：你觉得"塞翁失马，焉知祸福"的说法有道理吗？

生词

塞翁	名	Sàiwēng	An old man of the border
边塞	名	biānsài	border
纷纷	副	fēnfēn	in succession
惋惜	动/名	wǎnxī	sympathy, commiserations
不以为然	动	bùyǐwéirán	disagree
果然	副	guǒrán	sure enough
灾祸	名	zāihuò	disaster and misfortune
兜风	动/名	dōufēng	have a ride
飞驰	动/名	fēichí	run quickly
残疾	名	cánjí	disabled
闻讯	动	wénxùn	on hearing the news
大举	副	dàjǔ	on large scale, massive
身强力壮	形	shēnqiánglìzhuàng	strong and healthy
入侵	动/名	rùqīn	invade
征	动	zhēng	recruit, levy
十有八九	副	shíyǒubājiǔ	nine out of ten
服兵役	名	fúbīngyì	compulsory army service
灾难	名	zāinàn	disaster
焉	助	yān	how

幽默

肯德基店里的WE DO CHICKEN RIGHT该怎么翻译？

我们做鸡是对的；我们就是做鸡的；我们有做鸡的权利；我们只做鸡的右半边；我们可以做鸡，对吧?!；我们行使了鸡的权利；我们只做右边的鸡……；我们让鸡向右看齐；我们只做正版的鸡；只有朝右才是好鸡吧；我们有鸡的权利；只有我们可以做鸡；我们公正地做鸡；我们"正在"做鸡；右面的鸡才是最好的；向右看，有鸡；我们的材料是正宗的鸡肉（麦当劳做的是盗版）；我们做的是"右派"的鸡（麦当劳做的是"左派"的鸡！）；我们只做右撇子鸡（要吃左撇子鸡请去麦当劳）……

第十七课　怎样在中国做生意—跨国企业成功案例

大　　卫：李老师，除了管理之外，有没有别的应该注意的问题？
李老师：有，广告就是一个值得重视的问题。广告中不能出现不尊重所在国文化和习俗的画面和词语。
玛　　丽：你能不能举一个例子？
李老师：好。日本丰田汽车的两则广告曾在中国引起了不小的风波。其中一则为一辆丰田汽车停在两只石狮子前，一只石狮子在敬礼，另一只石狮子低着头，广告语为"霸道，你不得不尊敬"。
玛　　丽：狮子在中国是权威的象征，狮子敬礼、低头非同小可。
李老师：你说得对。去年9月份的《国际广告》杂志刊登了一则立邦漆广告作品，画面上的左立柱色彩黯淡，龙紧攀其上；右立柱色彩光鲜，龙却跌落到地上。
大　　卫：龙是中国的象征，龙跌落在地肯定会伤害中国人的感情。
玛　　丽：是啊。立邦漆再厉害也不能把中国龙剥下来啊。
李老师：美国耐克公司篮球鞋广告片"恐惧斗室"最近也被停播。在广告中，身穿长袍中国人模样的老人、身穿中国服装的妇女和两条龙频频被美国巨星打败。
大　　卫：也许他们是无意中伤害了中国人民的感情。穿中国服装是为了让中国人感到亲切。
玛　　丽：为什么穿耐克的小伙子不是中国人？他穿上耐克后频频得胜。那样不更能唤起中国人的购买欲吗？
李老师：做广告无非是为了让顾客买你的产品。如果适得其反，不管是无意还是有意，在商务运作上都是失败。
大　　卫：李老师，有没有成功的例子？
李老师：有。可口可乐、宝洁和通用汽车公司都是成功的例子。
玛　　丽：可口可乐在中国很受欢迎。
李老师：可口可乐公司确实读懂了中国文化。我们今天就来看一下可口可乐是怎样在中国获得成功的。

可口可乐在中国成功案例

全球最大的软饮料厂商可口可乐公司自1979年进入中国以来，已经建立了28家装瓶厂，总投资超过了11亿美元。中国已成为美国、墨西哥、德国、巴西、日本以外的第六大市场。

可口可乐在全球力推"本地化思维，本地化营销"的市场策略，以本土的思维方式看问题并与当地环境相融合。这种手法有力地推动了营销。2000年，可口可乐将中国区总部从香港迁到了上海，98%的原材料实现了当地采购。2002年，公司首次任命了三位中国本土人士担任副总经理。为了更好地适应中国市场竞争的需要，可口可乐还于2003年2月18日正式启用了中文新标识。

可口可乐是最早在当地制作电视广告的公司之一。公司要求广告要同当地人民的情感融为一体。2001年春节公司推出阿福阿喜新年特别包装，以新年吉祥的本土形象出现在电视广告上。这是可口可乐继"大风车"、"舞龙"广告之后的第三部专为中国市场推出的"新年贺岁广告"。可口可乐包装瓶上的两个儿童正是人们熟悉的泥娃娃阿福和阿喜，他俩怀抱可口可乐瓶，笑容可掬。背景颜色以红色为主，夹杂有明黄色。红色代表可口可乐，明黄色代表中国。

非常中国化的木偶形象阿福和阿喜的出现，引起了大众共鸣，人们从心理上认同可口可乐的新包装。该广告片通过贴春联和放烟花等行为形成可口可乐和大家一起过春节的感觉。在中国人全家团圆的日子里，可口可乐用家庭形象推广2.25升的包装。全家福的形象暗示着产品的对象，而2.25升更适合请客吃饭时候的饮料消耗量。所以这个广告体现出进入中国市场20多年后，可口可乐已经成为中国人生活中的一部分，而中国化的可口可乐肯定在中国更好卖。可口可乐公司还在中国内地推出了一套十二生肖的易拉罐，据说是全球首次中国主题的一套纪念品，惹得香港的朋友都从北京成箱地运可乐。

可口可乐深知，光占领中国人的胃不行，还要占领中国人的心。因此可口可乐积极参与各项公益活动，在农村兴建希望小学和希望图书库，在城市赞助青少年体育运动。在中国申奥成功的消息传出不到半小时的时间内，3万箱为此特别设计的奥运金罐就从北京可口可乐有限公司的生产线上下线，并连夜送往各大商场和零售摊点。

生词

画面	名	huàmiàn	picture, scene
霸道	形	bàdào	overbearing, high-handed
权威	名	quānwēi	authority
象征	名	xiàngzhēng	symbols
非同小可	形	fēitóngxiǎokě	no small matter
紧攀其上	动	jǐnpānqíshàng	firmly attached to it
剥	动	bō	peel off, throw off
恐惧	名	kǒngjù	fear
斗室	名	dǒushì	small room or dwelling
长袍	名	chángpáo	long gown (traditional scholar's garment)
唤起	动	huànqǐ	raise, awake, kindle
迁	动	qiān	move
暗示	动/名	ànshì	imply, hint
标识	名	biāoshí	mark, sign
吉祥	形	jíxiáng	auspicious, lucky
贺岁	名	hèsuì	celebration of the New Year
笑容可掬	形	xiàoróngkějū	wreathed in smiles, beaming
夹杂	动	jiāzá	mixed with
木偶	名	mù'ǒu	puppet, doll

春联	名	chūnlián	Spring Festival couplet
共鸣	名	gòngmíng	resonance, sympathetic response
消耗量	名	xiāohàoliàng	consumption amount
易拉罐	名	yìlāguàn	easy open can (for drinks)
纪念品	名	jìniànpǐn	souvenir
公益	名	gōngyì	for the benefit of public
赞助	名/动	zànzhù	sponsor
申奥	名	shēn'ào	bid to host Olympic Games
色彩黯淡	形	sècǎi'àndàn	with dark and dull colours
适得其反	动	shìdéqífǎn	run counter to one's desire

专有名词

丰田	Fēngtián	Toyota
立邦	Lìbāng	Nippon
耐克	Nàikè	Nike
宝洁	Bǎojié	Procter & Gamble
通用汽车	Tōngyòngqìchē	General Motors
墨西哥	Mòxīgē	Mexico
巴西	Bāxī	Brazil
阿福	Āfú	New Year good luck figurine of young boy
阿喜	Āxǐ	New Year good luck figurine of young girl

注释

1. 引起……风波：cause a stir or disturbance。

    例句： 1）水门事件当时在美国引起了一场很大的风波。

    2）他的一番话在公司里引起了一场不必要的风波。

2. 再……也不能：however … it shouldn't …

    例句： 1）你再恨他也不能见死不救啊！

    2）我再笨也不能连这个也不知道啊。

3. **再厉害也不能**：厉害 is a colloquial term implying formidable in both a good and bad sense.

　　例句： 1） 你别理他，他很厉害，对谁都很不客气。(awful)
　　　　　 2） 她那张嘴可厉害了，谁也说不过她。　　(sharp-tongued)
　　　　　 3） 他很厉害，什么难事他也能解决。　　　(capable)

4. **无意**：have no intention, accidental

　　例句： 1） 我在无意中发现了他的秘密。
　　　　　 2） 说者无意，听者有心。

5. **无非**：nothing but, no more than

　　例句： 1） 她学习中国烹饪无非是想讨好她的中国男朋友。
　　　　　 2） 降价处理无非是为了资金周转。

练习

一、根据课文判断正误

1. 广告中不能出现不尊重所在国文化和习俗的画面和词语。
2. 狮子在西方是权威的象征，在中国不是。
3. 龙跌落在地肯定会伤害中国人的感情。
4. 无意中犯的错误没什么关系。
5. 中国已成为可口可乐的第六大市场。
6. 可口可乐是最早在当地制作电视广告的公司之一。
7. 可口可乐任命了三位外国人士担任中国地区副总经理。
8. "大风车""舞龙"都是可口可乐为中国市场推出的广告。
9. 可口可乐在香港推出了一套十二生肖的易拉罐。
10. 中国人都很喜欢可口可乐的新年特别包装。
11. 可口可乐的包装背景颜色以绿色为主。
12. 该广告有贴春联、放烟花等中国人过春节的行动。

13. 可口可乐在中国兴建希望小学和希望图书库。
14. 可口可乐没有在中国赞助青少年体育运动。
15. 可口可乐的成功是由于公司确实读懂了中国文化。

二、评论下列广告

顾客：一个星期就好了，一个星期……

（老板摇头）

顾客：三天时间，三天时间好不好？

老板：（态度坚决）我说了多少遍了，我们的优惠期已经过了。

顾客：大哥，大哥啊……(跪地拉着老板的裤管乞求)。

旁白：幸好麦当劳了解我错失良机的心痛，给我365天的优惠……

三、根据词义连线

色彩黯淡　　　　　　　　颜色又明又亮
色彩光鲜　　　　　　　　不是一件小事
体现出　　　　　　　　　恰恰相反的结果
融为一体　　　　　　　　大众受益的活动
霸道　　　　　　　　　　表现出
公益活动　　　　　　　　成为一个整体
非同小可　　　　　　　　做事专横
适得其反　　　　　　　　颜色又暗又浅

四、根据词语搭配连线（可以有多种搭配）

停止　　　　　　　　　　播放
引起　　　　　　　　　　土地
唤起　　　　　　　　　　广告
刊登　　　　　　　　　　摊点
占领　　　　　　　　　　方式
零售　　　　　　　　　　共鸣
思维　　　　　　　　　　感情
伤　　　　　　　　　　　购买欲

五、用下列词语造句

1. 无意
2. 再……也不能
3. 与……相融合
4. 无非
5. 引起……风波

六、选词填空

1. 今年国庆的时候，我们去天安门广场看_____烟花。　　　（打/放）
2. 我们的这次比赛是由汉办_____的。　　　　　　　　　　（赞助/赞扬）
3. 每年春节，我们家都_____春联。　　　　　　　　　　　（挂/贴）
4. 贝克汉姆宣布不在_____英格兰足球队的队长了。　　　　（担任/担当）
5. _____汽车深受工薪阶层的欢迎。　　　　　　　　　　　（本土/本来）
6. 失败_____是世界的末日。　　　　　　　　　　　　　　（并非/无非）
7. 红色月季_____爱情。　　　　　　　　　　　　　　　　（形象/象征）
8. 学校新的网址今天_____。　　　　　　　　　　　　　　（使用/启用）
9. 儒家文化对中国人民的_____方式产生了巨大的影响。　　（思维/思想）
10. _____就是亲人之间的感情。　　　　　　　　　　　　　（亲情/亲切）

11. （永远、区别、必然、爱心、努力、同样、红光满面、面黄肌瘦、相互、带）

　　天堂与地狱的区别：一个人不知道天堂与地狱的_____，于是他去问上帝。上帝先_____他去了地狱，他看到所有人都是_____。他们面前都是美食，每个人手里都拿着一双长长的筷子，很多人都在_____地往自己嘴里送，但是筷子太长了，_____都送不进嘴里。上帝又带他去了天堂，天堂里的人_____。每个人手里拿着_____的长筷子，自己送不到自己嘴里，他们就两个人_____喂食。其实天堂与地狱的区别就是：只要人人都有_____，都有替别人着想的责任心，生活就_____是美好的！

七、讨论题

1. 你认为在跨文化企业发展中主要的成功因素有哪些？
2. 谈谈你对广告作用的看法。

阅读理解

两个老太太的故事

一个中国老太太和一个美国老太太在天堂相遇，谈起了在人间的一生。美国老太太说："我辛苦了三十年，终于把住房贷款都还清了。"中国老太太说："我辛苦了三十年，终于攒够了买房的钱。"美国老太太在自己买的房子里住了三十年，而中国老太太刚攒够了买房的钱，却去了天堂，无福享受自己买的新房。

美国老太太去世以后，她的子女办完了丧事就去了银行贷款买新房。于是就像他们的母亲一样，开始了漫长的还款历程。中国老太太去了天堂以后，她的子女说："母亲真好，辛苦了一辈子，给我们留下了一套新房。我们也要努力攒钱，给我们的孩子买新房子。"于是开始了攒钱的漫长历程。

于是，美国人在用餐前要祷告："感谢主，赐给我衣服，赐给我食物。"中国人在用餐前，在祖先灵位前点上一炷香，烧上几张纸钱，供上热腾腾的饭食，然后自己用餐。美国人感恩上帝，中国人尊祖。"祖先"是一个不断增加的序列，现在活着的人将来也会成为这个序列中的一分子，所以中国人崇尚伦理亲情。

思考：这个故事在你和中国人做生意时对你有什么帮助？

生词

辛苦	名/形	xīnkǔ	(endure) hardship, toil
攒	动	zǎn	accumulate, save up
无福	形/副	wúfú	not have the good fortune
历程	名	lìchéng	course
一辈子	名	yībèizi	whole life
赐给	动	cìgěi	bestow
祖先	名	zǔxiān	ancestors
灵位	名	língwèi	memorial tablet (with name of deceased)
一炷香	名	yīzhùxiāng	a stick of incense
供上	动	gòngshàng	offer up
热腾腾	形	rètēngtēng	steaming hot
感恩	动	gǎn'ēn	feel grateful
尊祖	动	zūnzǔ	worship ancestor
序列	名	xùliè	sequence
崇尚	动	chóngshàng	respect, esteem
伦理	名	lúnlǐ	ethics, moral principles

幽默

入乡随俗

爱默生教授应邀到某裸体俱乐部发表演讲，车到俱乐部门前时看见门上挂着一块牌子"请入乡随俗，以免尴尬"。于是，他停下车来，脱得一丝不挂。不料他进去时却发现，为了表示对他的尊敬，每个人都穿得很齐整。

第十八课　　介绍一个中国企业

玛　丽：李老师，毕业以后我想发挥我会说汉语的优势，到中国去工作或者到海外的中国跨国公司工作。

李老师：好哇。无论去哪儿，你的语言优势都会对你有很大帮助。

大　卫：我对中国的公司不太了解，好像中国的跨国企业不多。

李老师：你们都知道中国改革开放才二十多年，中国的跨国经营才刚刚起步，所以跨国企业比较少。

玛　丽：中国的国有企业比较有名，进入《财富》500强的中国企业差不多都是国有企业。

李老师：你说得没错。可是国有企业也在进行改革，实行股份制，也在招聘外国职工。你也可以去中国的国有企业工作。

玛　丽：我听说中国企业的工资比外企的低，不知道是不是真的这样。

李老师：真的是这样的。中国是发展中国家，工资及其福利待遇都不如发达国家。不过你可以去海外的中国企业工作，他们的工资都已经和所在国的工资接轨。

大　卫：李老师，能给我们介绍几个比较知名的中国企业吗？

李老师：好。汽车制造业有东风、上海大众汽车有限公司；银行业有中国银行、中国工商银行；饮食业有青岛啤酒股份有限公司等。

玛　丽：老师，哪一家公司最有名？

李老师：海尔。

大　卫：那是一家什么样的企业？

李老师：海尔是家电器生产厂家，2004年海尔蝉联中国最有价值品牌第一名。2004年1月31日，海尔入选世界品牌实验室编制的《世界最具影响力的100个品牌》，排在第95位，实现了中国品牌零的突破。

大　卫：这么厉害！海尔的企业管理一定很出色。

李老师：到目前为止，美国哈佛大学、瑞士洛桑国际管理学院、法国欧洲管理学院等七所商学院把海尔的管理模式作为教材，共做了十六个案例，涉及企业兼并、财务管理、企业文化等。

玛　丽：请您快快给我们介绍一下海尔吧。

海尔集团简介

海尔集团创立于1984年，20年来持续稳定发展，已成为海内外享有较高声誉的大型国际化企业集团，产品从1984年的单一冰箱发展到拥有白色家电、黑色家电、米色家电在内的96大门类、15100多个规格的产品群，并出口到世界160多个国家和地区。2004年，海尔全球营业额突破了1000亿元。

海尔集团已经建立起了一个具有国际竞争力的全球设计网络、采购网络、制造网络、营销与服务网络。现有工业园10个、海外工厂及制造基地30个、海外设计中心8个、营销网点58800个。海尔在中国家电市场上的整体份额已达到21%。海尔白色家电市场份额为34%，超过了国际公认垄断线。海尔小家电市场份额为14%，已经超越小家电传统强势品牌而位居第一。在国际市场上，海尔小冰箱和酒柜在美国占据市场份额第一；洗衣机在伊朗占据市场份额第一；空调在塞浦路斯占据市场份额第一。

海尔依据多年的实践经验，创造出了具有中国特色的OEC管理模式。"O"表示全方位，"E"表示每人、每天、每事，"C"表示控制和管理。其主要内容可以概括为：整个集团，每个人都处理好每天所发生的每件事情。

1998年8月海尔开始试点推行质量市场链管理模式，简称为"SST"制，SST是对OEC的改善和进一步提高。"SST"是索酬、索赔和跳闸三个名词汉语拼音第一个字母。索酬就是通过服务获得报酬；索赔就是部门之间如果不能履约，就要遭到索赔；跳闸就是在既不索酬、也不索赔的情况下，第三方就会自动"跳闸"。SST将企业内部的各个生产工序以及每个员工都纳入了市场的全方位控制之中。同时也将每个员工的收入纳入了市场的调节范围。这极大地激发了员工的积极性和潜力，提高了整个企业的活力和水平。海尔的管理充分体现了以人为本的管理思想。

生词

招聘	动	zhāopìn	recruit
福利待遇	名	fúlìdàiyù	social benefits, welfare benefits
接轨	动	jiēguǐ	come into line with
饮食业	名	yǐnshíyè	food and drink industry
蝉联	动	chánlián	retain, be awarded on successive occasions
编制	动	biānzhì	compile
营销网点	名	yíngxiāowǎngdiǎn	point of sale (in a network)
份额	名	fèn'é	(market) share
垄断	名/动	lǒngduàn	monopoly, monopolise
强势品牌	名	qiángshìpǐnpái	leading brand
概括	动	gàikuò	summarise, epitomise
市场链	名	shìchǎngliàn	market chain
索酬	动	suǒchóu	reward seeking
索赔	动	suǒpéi	compensation seeking
履约	动	lǚyuē	fulfil contract
激发	动	jīfā	stimulate

专有名词

海尔	Hǎi'ěr	Haier (a major Chinese home appliance producer)
中国银行	Zhōngguó yínháng	Bank of China
中国工商银行	Zhōngguó gōngshāng yínháng	Industrial and Commercial Bank of China
东风汽车股份有限公司	Dōngfēng qìchē gǔfèn yǒuxiàn gōngsī	Dongfeng Automobile Co. Ltd
上海大众汽车有限公司	Shànghǎi dàzhòng qìchē yǒuxiàn gōngsī	Shanghai Volkswagen Co. Ltd
青岛啤酒股份有限公司	Qīngdǎo píjiǔ gǔfèn yǒuxiàn gōngsī	Tsingtao Brewery Company Limited
伊朗	Yīlǎng	Iran
塞浦路斯	Sàipǔlùsī	Cyprus
哈佛大学	Hāfó dàxué	Harvard University
瑞士洛桑国际管理学院	Ruìshì luòsāng guójì guǎnlǐ xuéyuàn	Institute for Management Development, Lausanne

注释

1. **家电可以分为三类**：白色家电、黑色家电和米色家电。

   白色家电指电冰箱、洗衣机等可以替代人们劳务的产品；

   黑色家电指电视、音响等可以提供娱乐的产品；

   米色家电指电脑信息产品。

2. **发挥……优势**： play to ones strengths…

   例句： 1）我们应该发挥我们的语言优势，进军中国市场。

   2）只有发挥自己的优势，企业才能在竞争中生存发展。

3. **和……接轨**： in line with

   例句： 1）中国经济正处于和国际接轨的进程中。

   2）汽油价和国际接轨了，可是工资并没有接轨。

4. **实现……的突破**： to achieve a breakthrough in

   实现中国品牌零的突破：to have a breakthrough in that a Chinese brand has for the first time entered the list of the world's 100 top brand names.

   例句： 1）中国载人飞船的试飞成功，标志着中国的航天工业实现了历史性的突破。

   2）克隆技术的成功实现了生命科学上的重大突破。

练习

一、根据课文判断正误

1. 进入《财富》500强的中国企业差不多都是国有企业。
2. 国有企业不可以实行股份制。
3. 中国企业的工资比外企的低。

4. 海尔排在《世界最具影响力的100个品牌》的第55位。
5. 海尔是一家电器生产厂家。
6. 青岛啤酒是中国最有价值品牌第一名。
7. 海尔的管理模式已成为瑞士洛桑国际管理学院的教案。
8. 海尔从生产电冰箱开始。
9. 海尔的产品出口到世界160多个国家和地区。
10. 海尔在中国家电市场的整体份额已达50%。
11. 海尔白色家电在中国最受欢迎。
12. 海尔的产品在美国市场不太受欢迎。
13. 海尔的OEC管理模式，"O"表示全方位，"E"表示每人、每天、每事，"C"表示中国。
14. 1998年8月海尔开始试点推行质量市场链管理模式。
15. "SST"是质量市场链管理模式的英文缩写。

二、知识问答

1. 讲解下列图表

海尔发展战略创新的四个阶段

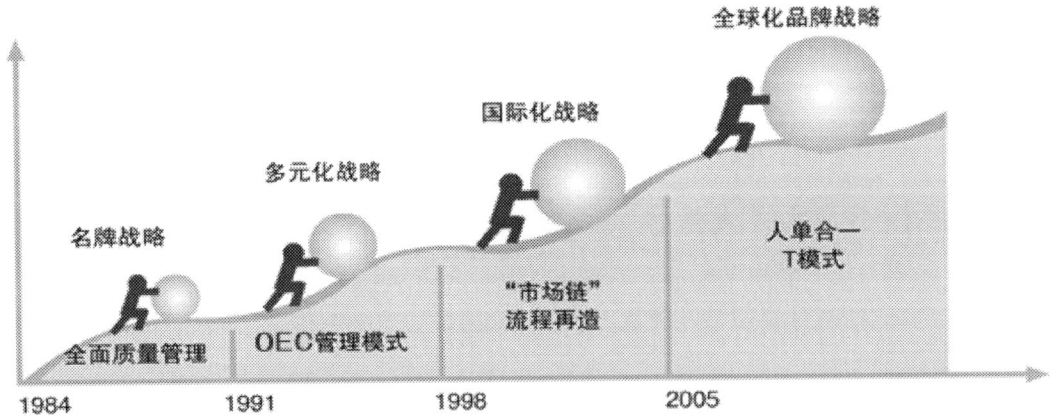

2. 写出下列公司的英文名字　　参考网站：www.google.com

英国石油　　　　　　　　汇丰控股
沃达丰　　　　　　　　　苏格兰皇家银行
保诚　　　　　　　　　　巴克莱银行

葛兰素史克	英国电信
希尔顿集团	皇家太阳保险
联合利华	皇家壳牌石油
玛莎	乐购
菲亚特	皇家飞利浦电子
松下电器	索尼
三洋	东芝
日立	佳能
富士胶片日本	柯达
三菱汽车	本田汽车
马自达汽车	铃木汽车
现代汽车	三星电子

三、根据词义连线

声誉	服务的网状覆盖点
市场份额	对钱财的管理
服务网络	用于娱乐的电器
财务管理	名誉和声望
产品规格	产品规定的标准
米色家电	电脑等信息类电器
黑色家电	洗衣机等家用电器
白色家电	在市场总份数中所占的比例

四、反义词连线

优势　　　　　　　　具体

稳定　　　　　　　　竞争

招聘　　　　　　　　无限

履约　　　　　　　　劣势

有限　　　　　　　　违章

获得　　　　　　　　波动

垄断　　　　　　　　丧失

概括　　　　　　　　解雇

五、用下列词语造句

1. 招聘
2. 激发
3. 发挥……优势
4. 突破
5. 与……接轨

六、选词填空

1. 欧盟加大对_____行为的惩罚力度。　　　　　　（垄断/截断）
2. 汉语教学已经被_____这个国家的中学教育。　　（纳入/进入）
3. 我们公司提供_____担保业务。　　　　　　　　（赴约/履约）
4. 这个产品的_____手册可以从网上下载。　　　　（规定/规格）
5. 这个款式充分体现了你青春的_____。　　　　　（活力/火力）
6. 大家都_____巴西足球队的势力很强。　　　　　（公认/认识）
7. 你可以给我打电话_____发电子邮件。　　　　　（还是/或者）
8. 这个产品的制作要经过十五道_____。　　　　　（工程/工序）
9. 北京出租车的_____费上涨了。　　　　　　　　（起步/起始）
10. 对方告我们违约，向我们_____。　　　　　　　（索赔/赔偿）

11．（文明、善于、不足、特点、自己、把握、影响着、讲究）

中国是一个_____古国，有五千多年的历史。传统儒家文化一直深深地_____中国人。儒家讲究礼仪，_____仁爱，讲究自我修养，这就造成了中国人在申请工作时不_____推销自己，怕别人以为是自吹，不够谦虚。而在西方，这种谦虚被认为是自信心_____，很难找到工作。同样，如果一位中国员工对某项工程有100%的_____时，他一般会说他只有80%的把握。这就是中国人的_____，总是不把话说绝，总是给_____留有后路。

七、讨论题

1．海尔为什么能获得成功？

2．你们国家里有中国跨国公司吗？如果有的话，请介绍一下。如果没有，请介绍一个你熟悉的中国公司。

阅读思考

宋清卖药

长安城里有一位人人皆知的药商,叫宋清。宋清待人仁厚,药的质量也好,所以远近闻名。凡是到他这里来卖药材的都知道宋清的人品好,价格合理,而且对送药材的人十分客气,热情地款待他们,请他们吃饭,远道来的还安排在自己家里休息过夜。所以,采药人都争先恐后到他那里卖药。

宋清的药好,来他这儿买药的人自然就很多。加上宋清卖药,如果对方一时无钱付账,可以欠账。宋清总是说:"治病救人要紧,什么时候有钱再送来就是了。"

人们因此十分赞赏他的人品。有的人家药费拖了一年,仍无钱付账,宋清也从不上门讨账。每到年底,宋清总要烧掉一些还不起钱的欠条。有人对此很不理解,说:"宋清这人一定是脑袋有问题,否则,怎么会做这样的傻事?"

宋清却说:"我并不觉得自己傻,我卖药挣钱不过是为了挣钱养家,我现在生活得很好不就行了。卖药40多年,我烧掉别人的欠条数不清。这些人大部分不是赖账,有的人后来有了钱,加倍地送钱给我,真正不还的毕竟是少数。如果像有些商人,对欠账的人不依不饶,怎么会有这么多的买主上门求药?人品是最好的宣传,人们对你信任,才会有事来找你,而不找别人,这是多少钱都买不来的信任。"

宋清以其高尚的人品,赢得了众人的敬重,他的生意也就越做越大,成了有名的富商。

思考:宋清卖药的故事对现代企业管理和经营有什么启示?

生词

人人皆知	形	rénrénjiēzhī	known to everyone
待人仁厚	动	dàirénrénhòu	treat people well
远近闻名		yuǎnjìnwénmíng	famous far and near, widely renowned
款待	动/名	kuǎndài	treat hospitably; entertain
争先恐后	副	zhēngxiānkǒnghòu	vie with one another to do sth.
欠账	动	qiànzhàng	put on account
赞赏	动/名	zànshǎng	praise, regard highly
讨账	动	tǎozhàng	seek payment, chase up bills
欠条	名	qiàntiáo	bill, account due for payment
赖账	动	làizhàng	repudiate a debt, refuse to pay
不依不饶	副/形	bùyībùráo	show no mercy, not let people off
宣传	名/动	xuānchuán	advertisement, publicity

幽默

推销良机

汽车商对自己的推销员说:"我想,这是你向鲍威尔推销一辆新轿车的最好时机。"

推销员颇为不解,问:"这是为什么呢?"

经理说:"别忘了他是个好胜的人,而他的邻居刚刚买了一辆新轿车。"

第十九课　参加博览会

大　　卫：我毕业后想自己成立公司跟中国人做贸易。李老师，如果跟中国人做贸易，就得了解他们的产品，我们通过什么样的手段来了解他们的产品最好？

李老师：现代社会信息非常发达，你可以通过访问供应商和厂商、参加博览会、甚至通过互联网来得到这方面的信息。

玛　　丽：我认为参加博览会是个好主意，你可以同时看到很多同类产品，这有利于我们的价格谈判。

李老师：你说得对。中国每年都举办各种规模和类型的博览会、展览会和洽谈会。著名的中国进出口商品交易会每年春秋举办两次，由于在广州举办，又称广交会。

大　　卫：我听说过。广交会的规模最大、商品最齐全。

李老师：其展场面积达540,000平方米。2004年春交会展位数量27,500个，展品种类超过15万种，成交额达245亿多美元，到会国家和地区203个，参展商数量12,224家。

玛　　丽：哇，真够大的了！广交会什么时候举办？

李老师：广交会一年两届，每届两期。春交会：第一期 4月15日－20日；第二期 4月25日－30日；秋交会：第一期 10月15日－20日；第二期 10月25日－30日。

大　　卫：广交会只做出口生意吗？

李老师：广交会原来以出口贸易为主，现在也做进口生意，还可以开展多种形式的经济技术合作与交流，以及商检、保险、运输、广告、咨询等业务活动。广交会贸易方式灵活多样，除传统的看样成交外，还举办网上交易会。

玛　　丽：那我们怎么申请参加广交会呢？

李老师：你可以从网上下载申请表格。申请得到批准后，你会收到邀请信，然后你携带邀请信去中国大使馆办签证就行了。

大　　卫：我主要想进口一些日用消费品，有没有专门这样的博览会？

李老师：有。我给你介绍一下义乌国际小商品博览会。

中国义乌国际小商品博览会

中国义乌国际小商品博览会（简称义博会）是唯一经过中国国务院批准的日用消费品类国际性博览会。义博会创办于1995年，到目前为止，已经成功举办了9届，是目前中国最具规模、最有影响、最有成效的小商品专业展会。

义乌地处浙江省，是中国小商品城，现有营业面积100万平方米，商位4万余个。义乌汇集了28个大类20多万种小商品，几乎囊括了所有日用消费品，是亚洲地区最大的小商品流通中心、信息中心和展示中心，也是中国最大的小商品出口基地。

义博会展中心的展馆功能齐全，展品车辆均可直接进入各个展厅。布置合理的入口和八台自动扶梯可以方便快捷地迎送八方来客。每个展位都可接互联网及国际直拨长途电话，使来宾可以轻松置身于电子商务环境，世界浓缩于荧屏之间。

2004义博会展览总面积超过7万平方米，设有国际标准展位3000个。共有20多个国家、26个省、市的1790家企业参展，其中境外企业占20%左右，知名企业和名牌产品的参展比例在30%以上。在本届展会中，经贸展览洽谈成交额74.3亿元，其中外贸成交额5.63亿美元，占总成交额的62.9%。

2004年义博会分七个展馆，A、E馆为工艺品，B馆为皮具箱包和化妆品，C、D馆为精品，F馆为电子电器和针织辅料，G馆为家居用品、文休用品、日用五金和玩具。展会首次增设电子商务区，阿里巴巴、谷歌等23家国内外著名网站参展。

2004年，参加中国义博会的境外客商来自五大洲164个国家和地区，其中亚洲为62%，欧洲13%，美洲14%，非洲7%，大洋洲2%，其他地区为2%。

如果你要参加义务国际小商品博览会，请到网站下载申请表。

生词

博览会	名	bólǎnhuì	expo
洽谈会	名	qiàtánhuì	fair
齐全	形	qíquán	complete
参展商	名	cānzhǎnshāng	exhibitor
届	量	jiè	measure for events, meetings, etc.
商检	名	shāngjiǎn	commodity inspection
咨询	名/动	zīxún	consult, consultancy
下载	动	xiàzǎi	download
携带	名/动	xiédài	carry, take
汇集	动	huìjí	assemble, bring together
囊括	动	nángkuò	include, embrace
自动扶梯	名	zìdòngfútī	escalator
功能齐全	形	gōngnéngqíquán	complete functionality, fully equipped
快捷	形	kuàijié	speedy, swift
置身于	动	zhìshēnyú	place oneself in
电子商务	名	diànzǐshāngwù	e-business
浓缩于	动	nóngsuōyú	condense to, shrink to
荧屏	名	yíngpíng	monitor, screen (computer)
成交额	名	chéngjiāo'é	volume of business
皮具	名	píjù	leather products
箱包	名	xiāngbāo	cases and bags
精品	名	jīngpǐn	luxury goods
针织辅料	名	zhēnzhīfǔliào	supplementary knitting materials
灵活多样	形	línghuóduōyàng	flexible and varied
家居用品	名	jiājūyòngpǐn	household goods
文体用品	名	wéntǐyòngpǐn	cultural and sports goods
日用五金	名	rìyòngwǔjīn	everyday hardware goods
增设	动	zēngshè	install in addition to

专有名词

义乌	Yìwū	city in Zhejiang province
大洋洲	Dàyángzhōu	Oceania
阿里巴巴	Ālǐbābā	an online B2B website(http://china.alibaba.com)
谷歌	Gǔgē	Google

注释

1. 看样成交：conclude a deal after examining samples.

2. 世界浓缩于荧屏之间： the world is presented concisely on the screen.
   浓缩于…… means to be condensed in…, concentrated in

3. 通过……的手段：by means of …
   例句： 1）通过兼并的手段扩大市场份额是见效较快的方法之一。
   2）有些公司通过不正当的手段进行市场竞争。

4. 八方来客：guests from all corners of the world. In Chinese, one often hears 四面八方, which indicates from all directions with the speaker in the centre.
   例句： 1）今年的武术节吸引了八方来客。
   2）上海磁浮列车春节不休息，八方来客新年"飞一回"。

5. 置身于：place oneself in
   例句： 1）置身于桂林山水之中，我仿佛进入了仙境。
   2）置身于一个改革开放的年代，我们大有作为。

6. 汇集：assemble, bring together
   例句： 1）这本书汇集了一百多首世界名曲。
   2）昨天上千人汇集在摄政公园纪念伦敦连环爆炸一周年。

7. 灵活多样：flexible and varied
   例句： 1）中国政府采取了灵活多样的国际教育合作形式。
   2）促销的方式可以灵活多样，比如买一送一。

练习

一、根据课文判断正误

1. 通过互联网可以获得贸易的信息。
2. 参加博览会是个好主意，有利于价格谈判。
3. 著名的中国出口商品交易会每年春季举办一次
4. 由于在广州举办，中国出口商品交易会又称广交会。
5. 广交会是世界上规模最大、商品最齐全的交易会。
6. 2004年春交会展品种类超过15万种。
7. 2004年参加春交会的国家和地区有100多个。
8. 广交会不做进口生意。
9. 义博会是亚洲最有影响、最有成效的小商品专业展会。
10. 义乌地处广东省。
11. 义乌是中国最大的纺织品出口基地。
12. 义博会的展馆功能齐全，展品车辆可直接进入展厅。
13. 2004年义博会分七个展馆，可是没有电子商务区。
14. 参加义博会的境外客商都来自亚洲。
15. 申请参加广交会和义博会的表格可以从网上下载。

二、根据词义连线

成交额	询问、征求意见
流通中心	商品检查
洽谈	用电子形式做生意
标准展位	参加展览的卖方
电子商务	交易总数
参展商	符合一定标准的展览位子
咨询	商量谈判
商检	商品买卖流动的主要地方

三、根据词语搭配连线（可以有多种搭配）

灵活　　　　　　　　　五金
功能　　　　　　　　　电话
方便　　　　　　　　　多样
电子　　　　　　　　　齐全
轻松　　　　　　　　　商务
看样　　　　　　　　　快捷
直拨　　　　　　　　　成交
日用　　　　　　　　　愉快

四、用下列词语造句

1. 置身于
2. 汇集
3. 浓缩于
4. 灵活多样
5. 携带

五、选词填空

1. 我们公司的_____比较小，是个小型企业。　　　　　（规模/规则）
2. 二手房_____现在非常活跃。　　　　　　　　　　　（成交/交易）
3. 心理_____在中国还没有流行起来。　　　　　　　　（咨询/问询）
4. 我们要预订两个标准_____。　　　　　　　　　　　（展位/展品）
5. 法国_____欧洲中心。　　　　　　　　　　　　　　（在于/地处）
6. 罪犯使用了高科技_____作案。　　　　　　　　　　（手续/手段）
7. 你可以免费从这个网站_____英文歌曲。　　　　　　（下载/上载）
8. 商场里面就有一台_____取款机。　　　　　　　　　（自动/主动）
9. 这种药治疗胃痛很有_____。　　　　　　　　　　　（成效/成绩）
10. 我们公司是当地_____的一家咨询公司。　　　　　（独一/唯一）

11. （比如、核心、有利、符合、延迟、决定、解决、导致、必须、成交）

在一份报价中，价格术语是＿＿＿＿＿部分之一。因为采用哪一种价格术语，实际上就＿＿＿＿＿了买卖双方的责任和利润的划分。选择以FOB价＿＿＿＿＿，在运费和保险费波动的市场条件下对出口商＿＿＿＿＿，但是也有些被动的方面，＿＿＿＿＿：由于进口商＿＿＿＿＿派船，或因其它情况＿＿＿＿＿装船期延迟，就会使出口商增加仓储等费用的支出。在CIF价出口的条件下，船货衔接问题可以得到较好的＿＿＿＿＿。在一般情况下，只要出口商保证所交运的货物＿＿＿＿＿合同规定，只要所交的单据齐全、正确，进口商就＿＿＿＿＿付款。

六、应用写作练习

请写一份参加下列交易会的申请

第89届中国针棉织品交易会
时间：2007-3-16 --- 2007-3-18
地点：南京国际展览中心
展会规模：50000 平方米
展品范围：内衣产品类：基础内衣、暖棉内衣、时尚内衣、文胸内衣、儿童内衣、家居寝服。 家用纺织品类：卧室用纺织品；浴室、厨房、餐厅用纺织品；窗用纺织品；家居装饰用布；车用纺织品、家居用皮草制品；宾馆、饭店专用纺织品。 服饰产品类：休闲服装、羊绒羊毛衫、手套袜品、丝巾领带、运动服装、泳衣泳裤。 针织相关产品类：针织辅料、针纺机械、针纺产品设计。
联系人　　俞 芳　　　　　　　电子邮箱 *shanghai-yu@163.com*
电话 021-54378548　　　　　　传真 021-54378548
地址　　上海莲花南路1288弄88号302室

七、讨论题

1. 中国的小商品生产对中国的经济发展起到了什么作用？

2. 你认为参加交易会是否十分必要？

八、成语趣解连线

最怪的动物	天涯海角	to be extremely open-minded
最难做的饭	晴天霹雳	very learned
最有学问的人	一日三秋	substitute the fake for the genuine
最短暂的季节	偷梁换柱	impossible for lacking the most essential
最反常的气候	虚怀若谷	to gain big profits with a small capital
最遥远的地方	博古通今	sudden and unexpected
最宽广的胸怀	虎头蛇尾	barren land
最赚钱的生意	无米之炊	the ends of the earth
最厉害的贼	一本万利	fine start and poor finish
最荒凉的地方	不毛之地	days creep like years

小故事

司马光

司马光出生于公元1019年11月，是北宋时期著名的政治家、史学家。他小的时候，有一次跟小伙伴们在院子里玩耍。院子里有一口大水缸，有个小孩爬到缸沿上，一不小心，掉进了缸里。

缸大水深，眼看那孩子就要被淹死了。别的孩子都吓得一面哭喊，一面往外跑，去找大人来救。司马光却不慌不忙，顺手从地上拾起了一块大石块，使尽全力朝水缸砸去。"砰"的一声，水缸被打破了，缸里的水流了出来，缸里的孩子得救了。

阅读思考

一道受益终身的测试题

这是一家公司招聘新职员的一道测试题……

你开着一辆车,在一个暴风雨的晚上经过一个车站。有三个人正在等公共汽车。一个是快要死的老人,非常可怜。一个是医生,他曾经救过你的命,是你的大恩人,你做梦都想报答他。还有一个女人/男人,她/他是那种你做梦都想娶/嫁的人,也许错过了就再也没有机会了。但是,你的车只能坐得下一个人,你会如何选择呢?请解释一下你的理由。

老人快要死了,你应该先救他。然而,每个老人最后都只能把死作为他们的终点站。你先让那个医生上车吧,因为他救过你,你认为这是报答他的好机会。但是你可以在将来某个时候去报答他,因为一旦错过了眼前的这个机会,你可能永远也遇不到一个让你这么动心的人了。

在200个应征者中,只有一个人被雇佣了,他并没有解释他的理由,他只是说了以下的话:

"给医生车钥匙,让他带着老人去医院,而我则留下来陪我的梦中情人一起等公车!"

绝大部分人都认为以上的回答是最好的,但很少有人一开始就能想到这种回答。是否是因为我们从未想过要放弃我们手中已经拥有的优势(车钥匙)?有时,如果我们能放弃一些我们的固执、狭隘和一些优势,我们可能会得到更多。

思考:你会如何选择?请解释一下你的理由。

生词

受益终身	名	shòuyìzhōngshēn	benefit for life
测试	名	cèshì	test
可怜	名	kělián	pitiful
报答	名	bàodá	repay
嫁	动	jià	marry (for a woman – marry off)
娶	动	qǔ	marry (for a man – take home)
钥匙	名	yàoshi	key (to a lock)
放弃	动/名	fàngqì	give up
固执	形	gùzhí	stubborn
狭隘	形	xiá'ài	narrow (mind, view etc)

幽默

我只收现金

金钱，可以用来买房子，但是买不到一个家；可以用来买床，但是买不到睡眠；可以用来买钟，但是买不到时间；可以用来买书，但是买不到知识；可以用来买职位，但是买不到尊重；可以用来买药，但是买不到健康；可以用来买血，但是买不回生命；可以用来买性行为，但是买不到真爱。所以金钱不是万能的！我之所以告诉你这些，是因为我是你真正的朋友！而身为你的朋友，我要帮你找到真正的幸福。所以把钱都寄给我吧！不过，我只收现金！

第二十课　　全球化与中国经济之前景

玛　丽：李老师，我们的商务汉语课就要结束了，我很想了解一下全球化对中国经济的影响。

李老师：经济全球化的发展，增进了商品和服务的跨国贸易，加大了国际资本流动量。经济全球化为中国利用国际资金和市场提供了难得的新机遇，但同时也带来挑战。

大　卫：昨天英国广播公司报道，根据经济合作与发展组织发表的报告，2003年中国成为最大的外商直接投资接受国。

玛　丽：真的吗？我还以为是美国呢。

李老师：中国现在已经取代了美国。中国在2003年吸引了来自经济合作与发展组织成员国的530亿美元的投资。

玛　丽：中国加入了世界贸易组织以后，市场自由化程度不断提高，外国企业都更加密切地关注着中国的市场。

大　卫：外商投资以往只看中发展中国家廉价的劳动力等低成本优势，现在他们更看重中国这个庞大的国内市场吧？

李老师：对，现在外商来中国投资的主要目的，是想在这个巨大的潜在市场中占有一定份额，而不仅仅是把中国作为廉价生产基地。对于那些子公司遍布全球的大型跨国公司来说，尤其如此。

玛　丽：李老师，你刚才说经济全球化也给中国带来了挑战，你指的是什么？

李老师：中国是发展中国家，全球化会对发展中国家的民族企业和市场带来不同程度的冲击，经济可能会产生波动。

大　卫：中国经济的前景会怎么样？面对全球化的机遇与挑战，中国经济还会继续高速发展吗？

玛　丽：外国公司现在可以通过兼并等方式收购中国的企业，中国对外资依赖的程度加重，中国会不会出现泡沫经济？

李老师：中国政府已经采取了措施。2004年4月，中国政府开始实行宏观调控政策，经济局部性过热和结构性失衡的矛盾已有所缓解。

中国经济之前景

"和谐"理念催生中国经济积极变化

90年代以来，随着科学技术的飞速发展，国际分工不断加深，生产和资本的国际化不断加强，国际经济联系越来越密切。世界进入了全球化时代。

在过去的几年里，中国一直是世界上经济增长速度最快的主要国家。中国经济的快速增长吸引了许多外国投资和跨国企业进入中国市场。中国加入世贸组织后取消了外资并购的限制，政府支持和鼓励中央企业进行联合重组，积极引导中央企业的并购活动。中央企业最终将保留80至100家，主要集中在资源、能源、冶金、汽车等具有重要战略意义的领域。政府打算只培育和发展30至50家具有国际竞争力的大公司、大企业集团。目前中央企业有179家。

在国际上，中国目前是大多数亚洲国家经济增长的一个主要源泉。日本和韩国的工业品、越南和印度的农产品、新西兰和澳大利亚的畜牧业产品、中亚的石油、南亚的矿藏、东盟各国的原材料，各种产品都能够在中国找到市场。与此同时，中国向这些国家提供了巨大的商机，吸引了亚太地区大量闲置资本前往中国投资。中国的影响也越出了亚洲。巴西和阿根廷等国的对华经贸增长了四到六倍。中国的兴起不仅仅就亚洲而言，而是就世界范围而言。

中国经济取得这样的成绩实属不易。2004年以来，中国在经济快速增长中出现了一些不稳定和不健康因素。粮食播种面积连年减少，固定资产投资增长过猛。与此同时，煤、电、油、运全面趋紧。在中国经济发展的重要关口，中国政府决定加强宏观调控，着力解决上述的问题。一年多来的实践证明，中国政府的宏观调控不仅没有影响经济持续较快地发展，而且对保持国民经济的平稳发展起到了重要作用。这次宏观调控，中国政府在操作上坚持实事求是，十分注意调控力度、时机和节奏的把握。中国在宏观调控中灵活地运用经济手段，这充分显示了中国政府驾驭市场经济的能力越来越娴熟。

中国的经济发展还会面临一些困难和挑战，但是只要中国政府实行合理调控，加强各项宏观调控政策和措施的落实执行，中国的经济就会继续平稳高速地发展。

生词

取代	动/名	qǔdài	replace
廉价	形	liánjià	low cost; cheap
庞大	形	pángdà	enormous
民族企业	名	mínzúqǐyè	national industry
波动	动/名	bōdòng	be volatile, volatility
依赖	名	yīlài	dependence
泡沫经济	名	pàomòjīngjì	bubble economy
失衡	动/名	shīhéng	imbalance
缓解	动	huǎnjiě	reduce, mitigate
重组	动/名	chóngzǔ	restructure; restructuring
冶金	名	yějīn	metallurgy
培育	动/名	péiyù	nurture, foster
源泉	名	yuánquán	source
矿藏	名	kuàngcáng	mineral resources
闲置资本	名	xiánzhìzīběn	idle capital
实属不易	形	shíshǔbúyì	really difficult, truly impressive
播种面积	名	bōzhòngmiànji	area of cultivation

着力	副	zhuólì	forcefully
上述	形	shàngshù	above-mentioned
平稳	形	píngwěn	smooth and steady
实事求是	形/副	shíshìqiúshì	seek truth from facts, practical & realistic
节奏	名	jiézòu	rhythm
把握	动/名	bǎwò	grasp, seize
驾驭	动/名	jiàyù	control
娴熟	形	xiánshú	skilled, adept
落实执行	名	luòshízhíxíng	implementation

专有名词

经济合作与发展组织　　　　Jīngjì hézuò yǔ fāzhǎn zǔzhī
OECD (Organisation for Economic Cooperation and Development)

印度	Yìndù	India
新西兰	Xīnxīlán	New Zealand
澳大利亚	Àodàlìyà	Australia
阿根廷	Āgēntíng	Argentina

注释

1. **随着科学技术的飞速发展**：along with the rapid development of science and technology. 随着 along with…, accompanying…

    例句：　1）随着中国经济改革的深入，中国的非国有经济已经有了很大的发展。

    　　　　2）随着公司业务的发展，公司对资金周转的控制也变得越来越重要了。

2. **不仅仅就亚洲而言，而是就世界范围而言**：not only in Asia, but also as far as the world is concerned… 就…而言: as far as … is concerned

例句： 1）就公司而言，我们也不希望通过裁员来压缩开支。

2）就该产品而言，它对消费者已经没有吸引力了。

3. **与此同时**：at the same time

例句： 1）他以优异的成绩考上了清华大学，与此同时上海交通大学也录取了他。

2）近年来大学生就业非常难，与此同时，农村中学却严重缺乏师资。

练习

一、根据课文判断正误

1. 经济全球化的发展，加大了国际资本流动量。
2. 经济全球化为中国利用国际资金和市场提供了机遇。
3. 2003年中国成为外商直接投资第二大接受国。
4. 大部分跨国公司仅仅把中国作为廉价生产基地。
5. 全球化会对发展中国家的民族企业和市场带来冲击。
6. 中国经济局部性过热和结构性失衡的矛盾已有所缓解。
7. 政府不支持中央企业兼并。
8. 东盟各国的原材料和产品都能够在中国找到市场。
9. 中国的影响仅仅是在亚洲。
10. 中国的粮食播种面积连年增加。
11. 中国近来固定资产投资增长过猛。
12. 政府认为固定资产投资增长过猛没什么，不必采取措施。
13. 中国在宏观调控中灵活地运用了经济手段。
14. 中国的经济发展不会面临什么挑战。
15. 只要中国政府实行合理调控，中国的经济就会继续平稳高速地发展。

二、下面的表格说明了什么？

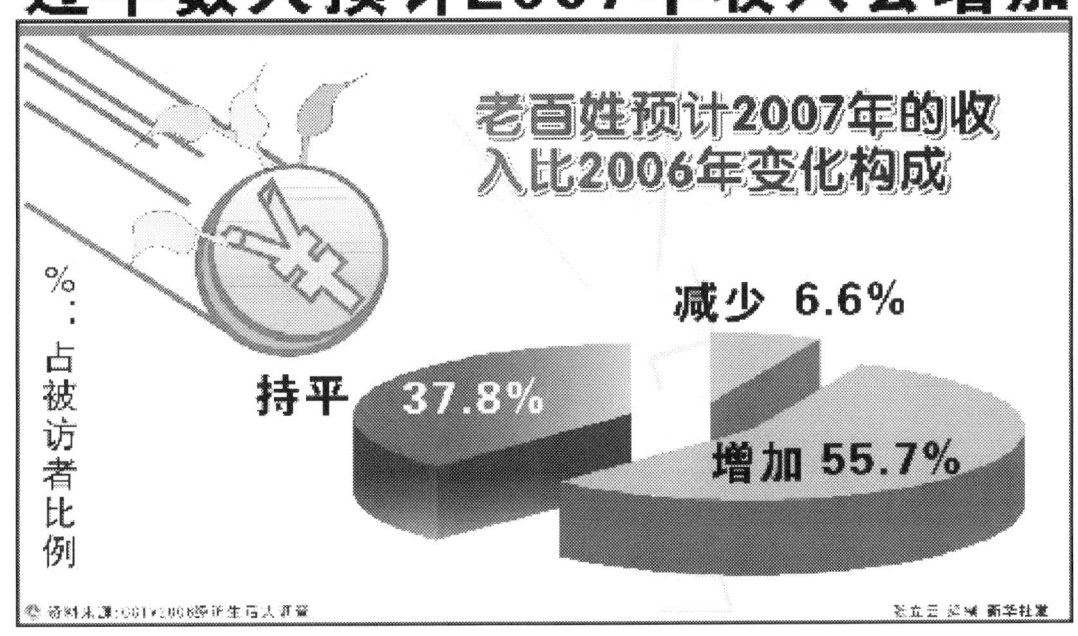

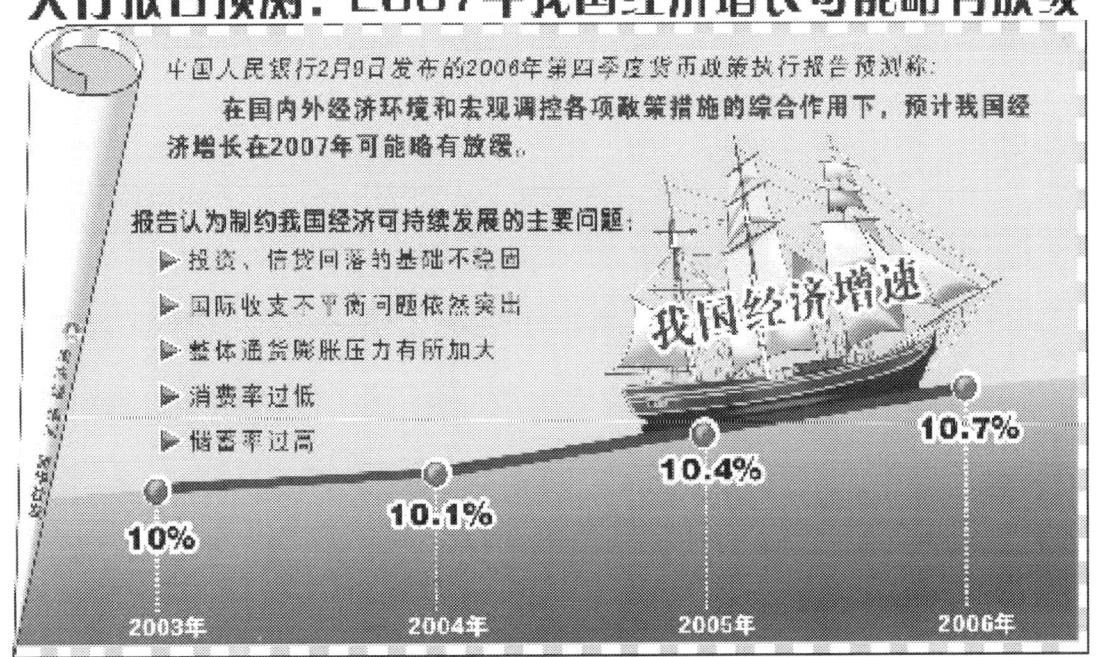

三、根据词义连线

原材料　　　　　　　　事物的原始点或来源
亟待解决　　　　　　　没有被使用的资金和设备
源泉　　　　　　　　　需要马上处理
外资并购　　　　　　　依靠外来资本运作的程度
泡沫经济　　　　　　　不以现金形式存在的资本
闲置资本　　　　　　　没有经过加工的东西
外资依赖度　　　　　　虚假的繁荣经济
固定资产　　　　　　　外来的买家出钱收购

四、同义词/近义词连线

机遇　　　　　　　　　依靠
廉价　　　　　　　　　停止
增进　　　　　　　　　促进
取代　　　　　　　　　培养
结束　　　　　　　　　巨大
庞大　　　　　　　　　机会
培育　　　　　　　　　便宜
依赖　　　　　　　　　代替

五、用下列词语造句

1. 就……而言
2. 娴熟
3. 实事求是
4. 与此同时
5. 取代

六、选词填空

（固定、操作、局部、着力、亟待、尤其、兴起、合理、以往、密切）

1. 我刚毕业，还没找到_____的工作。
2. 乡村旅游正在中国悄然_____。
3. 今年大学理科录取的分数线比_____高多了。
4. 上海今天_____有阵雨。
5. 我妈妈很喜欢看电视连续剧，_____是喜剧。
6. 公司正在_____解决环境污染问题。
7. 中国_____提高能源利用效率。
8. 银行电脑的_____系统出了问题，营业时间推迟了。
9. 目前人们都在_____关注二氧化碳排放量问题。
10. _____地避税不违法。

11. （调查、赚、发生、能力、合格、报告、于是、干、了解、所以）

　　这个故事_____在几年之前。我当时服务的那家公司是一家美国公司，对中国国情还不十分了解。一次，公司要在中国做市场_____。因为不相信中国有_____的市场调查公司，就请了一家欧洲调查公司去做。这家欧洲的公司没_____在中国做调查，一听是中国，心想中国是在亚洲，印度就是亚洲，_____就把活儿转包给一家印度公司。印度公司一想，中国，那是香港啊！于是就把活儿转包给一家香港公司。香港人是非常_____中国大陆的，于是把活儿转包给大陆一个很有名的市场调查公司。_____我去旁听的时候，见到了杂七杂八的一大堆人。钱是大家_____的，活儿是中国人_____的。最后的_____是欧洲人交的，内容是中国人做的。

七、讨论题

1. 你对中国经济发展之未来有何看法？
2. 你认为影响其发展的主要因素都有哪些？

阅读思考

两小儿辩日

大教育家孔子在周游列国时，有一次往东方的一个地方去，半路上看见有两个10岁左右的小孩在路边为一个问题争论不休，于是就让马车停下来，到跟前去问他们："小朋友，你们在争辩什么呢？"

其中一个小孩先说道："我认为太阳刚出来的时候离我们近一些，中午时离我们远些。"另一个小孩的看法正好相反，他说："我认为太阳刚升起来时远些，中午时才近些。"先说的那个小孩反驳说："太阳刚出来时大得像车盖，到了中午，就只有盘子那么大了。这不是远的东西看起来小，而近的东西看起来大的道理吗？"另一个小孩自然也有很好的理由，他说："太阳刚升起来时凉飕飕的，到了中午，却像是火球一样使人热烘烘的。这不正是远的物体使人感到凉，而近的物体使人觉得热的道理吗？"

两个小孩不约而同地请博学多识的孔子来做"裁判"，判定谁是谁非。可这个看似简单的问题却把孔老先生也难住了，因为当时自然科学还不发达，很难说明两个小孩的片面性，也就不能判断他们的谁是谁非了。孔子只好哑口无言。两个小孩都笑了起来，说："谁说你知识渊博，无所不知呢？你也有不懂的地方啊！"

这个故事给我们的启示是：从不同的角度会得出不同的看法，而要克服片面性就必须深化认识，进行辩证思维。

思考：这个故事给了我们什么样的启示？

生词

周游列国	动	zhōuyóulièguó	touring about different states
争论不休	动	zhēnglùnbùxiū	endless argument
争辩	动/名	zhēngbiàn	argue, debate
正好相反	形	zhènghǎoxiāngfǎn	just the opposite
反驳	动/名	fǎnbó	refute, criticise
车盖	名	chēgài	round chariot canopy
凉飕飕	形	liángsōusōu	chilly
热烘烘	形	rèhōnghōng	very warm, hot
物体	名	wùtǐ	object
不约而同	形/副	bùyuē'értóng	with one accord
博学多识	形	bóxuéduōshí	erudite
裁判	名	cáipàn	referee, judge
谁是谁非	形	shéishìshéifēi	who is right and who is wrong
片面性	名	piànmiànxìng	one-sidedness
哑口无言	名	yǎkǒuwúyán	speechless
知识渊博	形	zhīshiyuānbó	be erudite, have profound knowledge
无所不知	形	wúsuǒbùzhī	omniscient, know everything
深化	动	shēnhuà	deepen
辩证思维	名	biànzhèngsīwéi	dialectical thinking

幽默

成功的秘诀

一名记者采访某著名银行的总裁,想探知他成功的秘诀。

"你是如何获得成功的?"

"5个字——正确的决定!"

"怎样做出正确的决定?"

"2个字——经验!"

"怎样获得经验呢?"

"5个字——错误的决定!"

孔子及儒家思想

孔子

孔子（公元前551～前479）是春秋时期鲁国伟大的思想家、教育家，儒家学派的创始人。孔子，名丘，字仲尼，春秋晚期鲁国人（今山东曲阜市）。在中国封建社会里被尊为"圣人"。他出身于一个有贵族传统而已失掉贵族地位的家庭，生长在保存宗周典籍和文物制度最多、社会风俗古旧的鲁国，主要活动于社会大变动的时期。他做过大夫，而一生主要是从事私人讲学。相传有弟子三千，贤弟子七十二人。孔子曾带领弟子周游列国14年。晚年整理《诗》、《书》等古代典籍，删修《春秋》。孔子作为中国思想文化集大成者，他的哲学思想主要是提倡"仁义"、"礼乐"、"德治教化"，以及"君以民为体"。孔子的思想及学说对后世产生了极其深远的影响。孔子思想渗入了中国人的生活和文化领域，同时也影响了世界许多地区的人们近2000年。

儒家思想

儒家思想又称儒学，也有人认为它是一种宗教而称之为儒教。儒家思想由春秋末期思想家孔子创立。儒家思想是中国古代的主流意识流派，自汉以来在绝大多数的历史时期作为中国的官方思想，至今仍是中国社会一般民众的核心价值观，并在世界上作为中国文化的代表和民族传统的标记。

儒家哲学注重人的自身修养，要与身边的人建立一种和谐的关系。统治者要仁政爱民，为官者要清廉爱民。做人有自知之明，尽份内事。对待长辈要孝顺尊敬，朋友之间要真诚守信用。对待上司要忠诚，对待其他人要博爱。尊重知识，善于吸取别人的长处，提倡达到温、良、恭、俭、让的道德境界。"礼、义、廉、耻、仁、爱、忠、孝"的儒家思想基本价值观，一直是指导绝大部分中国人日常行为的基本意识规则。中华民族礼貌友善、温良忠厚和认真刻苦的气质，也是在儒家的教化下逐渐形成的。但儒学忽略了人的个性。这一点在后来发展得越来越严重。人文精神越来越淡薄，人的自身价值越来越被忽视和压制。

儒家思想不同于其它宗教。儒家思想关注的并非"自然"、"科学"，而是人和社会，在这些永恒的课题上，儒家思想建立起了具有永恒价值的价值体系。由于儒家文化只关心现世，将来世交给其他的宗教，因此对其他宗教有很大的宽容性。任何宗教，只要不试图干涉现世的政权，都可以在儒教的背景下存在。所以中国是历史上最早实行政教分离和宗教信仰自由的国家。在儒家文化圈内的历史上，从未发生过宗教战争，世界任何地区在宗教战争中失败的一方，都可以到中国继续传教、发展。儒家文化圈像一个黑洞，任何外来文化都会被吸收和消化，改造为本民族文化的组成部分。儒家文化不像西方文化那样主动扩张，而是一圈一圈地缓慢扩张，周围文化被同化的程度非常高。哪怕有很强主动性的基督教和伊斯兰教，到中国后，也很快被同化，和世界其他地区的教会有了很大的差异。

老子及道家思想

老子

老子（约公元前580～约前500年）是道家学派创始人。老子姓李名耳，今河南鹿邑人。老子是中国古代伟大的思想家、哲学家。老子曾为周做史官，管理藏书，后见周朝衰落，社会风气颓败，于是弃官归隐，归隐后著《老子》。《老子》又称《道德经》、《老子五千文》，是中国道家的主要经典。其中"道"的观念是其思想体系的核心。老子反对儒墨两派的道德观，认为真正道德是不追求道德，提倡柔弱虚静，减少私欲，知足不争。理想政治是无为而治，理想社会是小国寡民社会。老子死后，他的思想被战国时期的思想家庄子进一步发展。老子和庄子的思想成为后来道教哲学的主要思想，对中国历史影响十分深远。

道家思想

道家思想起始于春秋末期的老子。道家思想的核心是"道"，这一思想由天道演变而来，但与天道不同。老子提出"道"是宇宙的本源，也是统治宇宙中一切运动的法则。这一观点被后来所有道家流派支持，成为道家最基础的核心。各派之间对"道"的理解存在一定差异，但在中国哲学史上，通过"道"的概念对世界万物本源进行了第一次探讨，这是道家突出的贡献之一。

老子意识到，真实世界的主要特征是非永恒性，因而"道"是无法预先决定或者命名的，它与任何可命名的事物不同，然而它显然是真实的，并且是所有有限实在的根源。这里老子将非存在与存在的世界联系了起来，即非存在是永恒的，而存在是短暂和有限的。老子认为我们所感受到的自然都以"道"这样自发无为的方式运行的，自然也以此存在于"道"之中。

由于"道"存在于一切有限存在之中，人类本身也便是自然的显现。人们拥有生命，可以品味生活，但同时也要随时准备毫无遗憾地离开它，"道"所带给我们本身不可避免的病痛、死亡，都是自然有限存在的一个过程。对于生活方式，老子主张"仅仅活着"，强调"活着就行"。老子认为对人来说，欲望应是相当简单和有限的，然而现实现象是人的欲望很多。老子把它归结于两个因素：一是文明的兴起；二是人本身在道德层面上的堕落。

"无为"被道家认为是"道"的重要特征之一。它不是指不作为，而是指不经过深思熟虑、无目的地行为。道家认识到任何有目的的行为都可能使行为本身产生偏差。当我们提倡孝顺、和睦的时候，家庭中的成员可能已经不孝顺、不和睦了，不然是不需要这些的。表述类似观点的语句在道家的作品中随处可见。根据处理的问题不同，"无为"的态度即可用于政治，也可用于修身。

孙子及《孙子兵法》

孙子

孙子名孙武,字长卿。他出生于春秋后期的齐国,是中国古代著名的军事家,被尊为"兵家之祖"。孙武著有《孙子兵法》一书,共十三篇,流传至今。孙子出身贵族,这给他提供了优越的学习环境。他阅读了大量的古代军事典籍,加上当时战乱频繁,兼并激烈,他的祖父、父亲都是善于带兵作战的将领,这对少年孙武产生了深远的影响。他喜爱兵法,渴望探求战争中的制胜之道,以备将来点兵沙场,在战争舞台上干出一番惊天动地的事业来。然而孙武生不逢时,当时的齐国内部矛盾重重,危机四伏。孙武毅然告别齐国,投奔吴国。孙武一生事业都是在吴国展开的,死后也葬在了吴国。

《孙子兵法》

《孙子兵法》是世界上最早的兵书,也是中国兵学的奠基之作。《孙子兵法》充满了谋略的智慧。春秋战国时期,军事家常引用《孙子兵法》作为自己的军事行动的理论根据。汉代以后,《孙子兵法》更是被军事家视为指导战争的金科玉律,在整个冷兵器为主的漫长的历史时期,《孙子兵法》一直是军事家必读的教科书。不仅如此,《孙子兵法》所提出的原则和策略,还对政治、经济都有很大的指导作用。《孙子兵法》所提出的"全胜策"的思想,强调政治清明、君主贤明和内部团结的思想,发展统一战线、分化瓦解敌对势力等方面丰富的思想,丰富了中国古代政治学理论,受到历代政治家的重视。其战略战术思想,对于现实社会中商业竞争和其他方面的竞争,也具有指导意义。

《孙子兵法》不仅在中国产生积极影响,而且被先后译成多种语言,在世界上广泛流传。法国著名政治家、军事家拿破仑,在兵败滑铁卢之后,偶然得见《孙子兵法》,无限感慨地说:"如果二十年前能见到《孙子兵法》,历史将会是另外一个结局。"美国最著名的军校——西点军校,一直把《孙子兵法》定为必读教科书;许多日本企业家,都把《孙子兵法》作为商战指南。在1990年的海湾战争中,美国军队还将《孙子兵法》配备到人手一册,用来武装美国海军陆战队将官。随着时间的推移,《孙子兵法》还将进一步走向世界。

练习答案
Keys to the exercises

第十一课　孔子思想与企业管理

一、根据课文判断正误：

1. 误	2. 正	3. 正	4. 误	5. 正
6. 误	7. 正	8. 误	9. 正	10. 正
11. 误	12. 正	13. 误	14. 正	15. 误

二、知识问答

1. 孔子名丘，字仲尼，春秋后期鲁国人，今山东曲阜人。 2. C 3. B

三、根据词义连线

管理文化	管理实践和理论的综合表现
管理模式	管理的方式
管理理念	对管理的看法和观点
管理策略	管理的计谋
文化心理	受文化影响的思维和观念
文化震荡	对不同文化感到震惊
主导原则	用来指导实施的方针
趋同倾向	越来越相似、相近

四、根据词语搭配连线

取长补短、光辉灿烂、丰富多彩、恰到好处、
为人处事、互相借鉴、死守原则、团结合作

六、选词填空

1. 先后、文化、发行、国界、研究、其次、引起、模式
2. 请教、实施、品德、侮辱、获得、任用、取得、使唤

第十二课　老子思想与人力资源开发和管理

一、根据课文判断正误

1. 正	2. 误	3. 正	4. 误	5. 正
6. 正	7. 正	8. 正	9. 误	10. 正
11. 正	12. 正	13. 误	14. 误	15. 正

三、根据词义连线

听信逸言	相信别人说某人的坏话
埋没人才	不重视有才华的人
领导术	当老板的艺术
留有后路	留有回旋的余地
用其所长	使用他擅长的技能
忽视潜力	没有重视以后能够发挥的能力
贪公受贿	贪污公家的财产、接收他人给的钱财
善于卖弄	很会炫耀、显示自己

四、根据词语搭配连线
无所适从、真才实学、埋头苦干、自知之明、
当机立断、以身作则、赏罚分明、施展才能

六、选词填空
1. 即将、柔弱、张开、完全、胜、作为、容器、遇到、滴水、精神
2. 问、那么、挡住、背、储存、忍耐、脚掌、软软、原来、为什么

第十三课　孙子兵法与企业战略

一、根据课文判断正误

1. 正	2. 正	3. 误	4. 正	5. 正
6. 正	7. 误	8. 正	9. 误	10. 误
11. 正	12. 误	13. 正	14. 正	15. 正

三、根据词义连线

拙劣　　　　　　　　　　非常粗恶、非常笨
避实击虚　　　　　　　　躲开厉害的，打击软弱的
毫无信心　　　　　　　　一点儿信心也没有
后发制人　　　　　　　　等对方先动手，然后自己再反攻
三局两胜　　　　　　　　打三场赢了两场
知彼知己　　　　　　　　既了解自己也了解对手
错位竞争　　　　　　　　颠倒位置和对手比高低
相似之处　　　　　　　　差不多一样的地方

四、根据词语搭配连线
心慌意乱、目瞪口呆、赫赫有名、转败为胜、
运用计谋、古今中外、广为流传、得意洋洋

六、选词填空

1. 拍	2. 下	3. 指导	4. 摇头	5. 理
6. 挖苦	7. 古老	8. 毫无	9. 照样	10. 对策

11. 限制、交纳、想出、分别、作为、只好、傻瓜、早晚、注视、等待

第十四课　怎样和中国人做生意--商务习俗

一、根据课文判断正误

1. 误	2. 正	3. 误	4. 正	5. 误
6. 正	7. 正	8. 正	9. 误	10. 误
11. 正	12. 误	13. 误	14. 正	15. 正

三、根据词义连线

商务习俗　　　　　　　　　做生意的风俗习惯
入乡随俗　　　　　　　　　到一个地方要遵循这个地方的风俗
过分照顾　　　　　　　　　照料得太周全了
留面子　　　　　　　　　　不指出其错误或弱点
难堪　　　　　　　　　　　非常没面子
不忘前情　　　　　　　　　以前的情义一直记在心中
价格适中　　　　　　　　　价格不高不低，正合适
一时疏忽　　　　　　　　　偶尔不小心出错了

四、根据词语搭配连线

顾及对方/他人、贬低他人/对方、产生分歧、咂手指、
表示诚意/分歧、回请客人/对方/他人、吉利颜色、品尝食物

六、选词填空

1. 规定　　2. 诚意　　3. 讲究　　4. 回报　　5. 难堪
6. 过份　　7. 品尝　　8. 避免　　9. 产生　　10. 怀疑
11. 可是、期限、动静、意识到、废物、毫无、竞争、派去

第十五课　怎样在中国做生意 --人际沟通

一、根据课文判断正误

1. 正	2. 正	3. 误	4. 误	5. 正
6. 正	7. 误	8. 正	9. 误	10. 正
11. 正	12. 误	13. 误	14. 误	15. 正

三、根据词义连线

诉诸　　　　　　　　　　　求助于
大发雷霆　　　　　　　　　大发脾气，大声斥责
得罪人　　　　　　　　　　惹恼了他人
平息风波　　　　　　　　　把事态抑制住
明文规定　　　　　　　　　很清楚的书面规定
合二为一　　　　　　　　　将两者合为一个整体
所在国　　　　　　　　　　你目前逗留的那个国家
简而言之　　　　　　　　　简单地说

四、根据词语搭配连线

引起误会、等待机会、摆出事实、保养身体、
容忍体罚、保全面子、说明真相、维护权益

六、选词填空
1. 风波　　2. 侮辱　　3. 郑重　　4. 费劲　　5. 顶撞
6. 偏爱　　7. 毫无　　8. 得力　　9. 透明　　10. 编织
11. 担任、管辖、前任、因为、于是、治理、辛苦、借助、充分、团队

八、成语趣解连线

最高的人	顶天立地	upstanding and dauntless
最大的手	一手遮天	to hoodwink the public
最大的嘴	气吞山河	full of daring
最大的步	一步登天	to have a meteoric rise
最贵的字	一字千金	very precious
最尖的针	无孔不入	to seize every opportunity
最吝啬的人	一毛不拔	very stingy
最长的一天	度日如年	days wear on like years
最大的容量	包罗万象	all-inclusive
最快的速度	风驰电掣	extremely quick

第十六课　怎样在中国做生意 --跨国公司失败案例

一、根据课文判断正误
1. 正　　2. 正　　3. 误　　4. 正　　5. 正
6. 误　　7. 正　　8. 误　　9. 正　　10. 正
11. 误　　12. 误　　13. 正　　14. 误　　15. 正

二、知识问答
2. 写出下列公司的英文名字

沃尔玛	Wal-Mart	惠尔浦	Whirlpool
星巴克	Starbucks	百事可乐	Pepsi
强生	Johnson & Johnson	波音	Boeing
惠普	HP	戴尔	Dell
微软	Microsoft	摩托罗拉	Motorola
摩根士丹利	Morgan Stanley	花旗集团	City Group
摩根大通	JP Morgan	高盛集团	Goldman Sachs
美国运通	American express	美林国际	Merrill Lynch International
雪佛龙	Chevron	福特汽车	Ford
西门子	Siemens	宝马	BMW
汉莎集团	Lufthansa	欧莱雅	Loreal
家乐福	Carrefour	雷诺	Renault

标致	Peugeot	沃尔沃	Volvo
爱立信	Ericsson	诺基亚	Nokia
雀巢咖啡	Nescafe	瑞士信贷	Swiss Credit

三、根据词义连线

热情好客　　　　　　　　　对客人很友好，照顾得很周全
人心涣散　　　　　　　　　人心不齐
竞争对手　　　　　　　　　敌手
经验教训　　　　　　　　　从实践中得到的知识、技能或教悔
模式化经营　　　　　　　　以固定的方式运作
逻辑严密　　　　　　　　　条理性很强
狭隘民族主义　　　　　　　认为自己的民族又好又重要
周转不灵　　　　　　　　　不能正常调配

四、根据词语搭配连线

限制自由、委托制作、严格控制、跨国经营、
丢失商机、缺乏经验/商机、及时调整/报告、审批报告

六、选词填空

1. 紧凑　　2. 顺序　　3. 一贯　　4. 狭窄　　5. 景点
6. 经典　　7. 培训　　8. 执意　　9. 上乘　　10. 套用
11. 而、结果、观察、遭遇、检讨、至于、委屈、把握

第十七课　怎样在中国做生意 -- 跨国企业成功案例

一、根据课文判断正误

1. 正　　2. 误　　3. 正　　4. 误　　5. 正
6. 正　　7. 误　　8. 正　　9. 误　　10. 正
11. 误　　12. 正　　13. 正　　14. 误　　15. 正

三. 根据词义连线

色彩黯淡　　　　　　　　　颜色又暗又浅
色彩光鲜　　　　　　　　　颜色又明又亮
体现出　　　　　　　　　　表现出
融为一体　　　　　　　　　成为一个整体
霸道　　　　　　　　　　　做事专横
公益活动　　　　　　　　　大众受益的活动
非同小可　　　　　　　　　不是一件小事
适得其反　　　　　　　　　恰恰相反的结果

四、根据词语搭配连线
停止播放、引起共鸣、唤起购买欲/共鸣、刊登广告、
占领土地、零售摊点/方式、思维方式、伤感情

六、选词填空
1. 放　　2. 赞助　　3. 贴　　4. 担任　　5. 本土
6. 并非　　7. 象征　　8. 启用　　9. 思维　　10. 亲情
11. 区别、带、面黄肌瘦、努力、永远、红光满面、同样、相互、爱心、必然

第十八课　介绍一个中国企业—海尔公司简介

一、根据课文判断正误
1. 正　　2. 误　　3. 正　　4. 误　　5. 正
6. 误　　7. 正　　8. 正　　9. 正　　10. 误
11. 正　　12. 误　　13. 误　　14. 正　　15. 误

二、知识问答
2. 写出下列公司的英文名字

英国石油	BP	汇丰控股	HSBC
沃达丰	Vodafone	苏格兰皇家银行	Royal Bank of Scotland
保诚	Prudential	巴克莱银行	Barkley
葛兰素史克	GlaxoSmithKline	英国电信	BT
希尔顿集团	Hilton Group	皇家太阳保险	Royal & Sun Alliance
联合利华	Unilever	皇家壳牌石油	Shell
玛莎	Mark & Spencer	乐购	Tesco
菲亚特	Fiat	皇家飞利浦电子	Royal Philips
松下电器	Panasonic	索尼	Sony
三洋	Sanyo	东芝	Toshiba
日立	Nissan	佳能	Canon
富士胶片	Fuji film	柯达	Kodak
三菱汽车	Mitsubishi	本田汽车	Honda
马自达汽车	Mazda	铃木汽车	Suzuki
现代汽车	Hyundai	三星电子	Samsung

三．根据词义连线
声誉　　　　　　　　名誉和声望
市场份额　　　　　　在市场总份数中所占的比例
服务网络　　　　　　服务的网状覆盖点
财务管理　　　　　　对钱财的管理
产品规格　　　　　　产品规定的标准
米色家电　　　　　　电脑等信息类电器
黑色家电　　　　　　用于娱乐的电器
白色家电　　　　　　洗衣机等家用电器

四、反义词连线
优势 - 劣势、稳定 - 波动、招聘 - 解雇、履约 - 违章、
有限 - 无限、获得 - 丧失、垄断 - 竞争、概括 - 具体

六、选词填空
1. 垄断　　2. 纳入　　3. 履约　　4. 规格　　5. 活力
6. 公认　　7. 或者　　8. 工序　　9. 起步　　10. 索赔
11. 文明、影响着、讲究、善于、不足、把握、特点、自己

第十九课　参加博览会

一、根据课文判断正误
1. 正　　2. 正　　3. 误　　4. 正　　5. 正
6. 正　　7. 误　　8. 误　　9. 正　　10. 误
11. 误　　12. 正　　13. 误　　14. 误　　15. 正

三、根据词义连线

成交额	交易总数
流通中心	商品买卖流动的主要地方
洽谈	商量谈判
标准展位	符合一定标准的展览位子
电子商务	用电子形式做生意
参展商	参加展览的卖方
咨询	询问、征求意见
商检	商品检查

四、根据词语搭配连线
灵活多样、功能齐全、方便快捷/多样/成交、电子商务、
轻松愉快/多样/快捷、看样成交、直拨电话、日用五金

六、选词填空
1. 规模　　2. 交易　　3. 咨询　　4. 展位　　5. 地处
6. 手段　　7. 下载　　8. 自动　　9. 成效　　10. 唯一
11. 核心、决定、成交、有利、比如、延迟、导致、解决、符合、必须

八、成语趣解连线

最怪的动物	虎头蛇尾	fine start and poor finish
最难做的饭	无米之炊	impossible for lacking the most essential
最有学问的人	博古通今	very learned
最短暂的季节	一日三秋	days creep like years

最反常的气候	晴天霹雳	sudden and unexpected
最遥远的地方	天涯海角	the ends of the earth
最宽广的胸怀	虚怀若谷	to be extremely open-minded
最赚钱的生意	一本万利	to gain big profits with a small capital
最厉害的贼	偷梁换柱	substitute the fake for the genuine
最荒凉的地方	不毛之地	barren land

第二十课　全球化与中国经济之前景

一、根据课文判断正误

1. 正　　2. 正　　3. 误　　4. 误　　5. 正
6. 正　　7. 误　　8. 正　　9. 误　　10. 误
11. 正　　12. 误　　13. 正　　14. 误　　15. 正

三、根据词义连线

原材料	没有经过加工的东西
亟待解决	需要马上处理
源泉	事物的原始点或来源
外资并购	外国的买家出钱收购
泡沫经济	虚假的繁荣经济
闲置资本	没有被使用的资金和设备
外资依赖度	依靠外来资本运作的程度
固定资产	不以现金形式存在的资本

四、同义词/近义词连线

机遇 - 机会、廉价 - 便宜、增进 - 促进、取代 - 代替、
结束 - 停止、庞大 - 巨大、培育 - 培养、依靠 - 依赖

六、选词填空

1. 固定　　2. 兴起　　3. 以往　　4. 局部　　5. 尤其
6. 着力　　7. 亟待　　8. 操作　　9. 密切　　10. 合理
11. 发生、调查、合格、能力、于是、了解、所以、赚、干、报告

Confucianism and Business Management

Confucius is the founder of Confucianism and the creator of a set of Confucian doctrines whose ideas are reflected in a book called The Analects. There are a lot of ideas in Confucianism that can be utilised in business management.

"Benevolence" is the core of Confucianism. "Benevolence" means loving people. In the idea of "benevolence" advocated by Confucius there is a famous saying-"Do not do to others what you would not have done to yourself"This has been regarded by many businessmen as the "golden rule" for business management. There are also two other fundamental Confucian concepts. One is "prioritising people", and the other is "valuing harmony". "Harmony" refers to unity and cooperation between people. Conflicts and struggles often occur between individuals or between businesses. Confucians feel that "valuing harmony" should be given the highest priority in everything, as harmony is the basic principle for resolving conflict and sustaining development. Confucius very much stressed the role of "people" and "the hearts of the people" in the governance of the state, producing brilliant maxims, such as: "A just cause enjoys abundant support while an unjust cause finds little support", and "An auspicious time is not as important as an earthly advantage, but an earthly advantage is not as important as harmony amongst the people".

Confucius advocated using the "golden mean" to observe and to deal with nature and society. The idea of the "golden mean" has long been the guiding principle for Chinese people when dealing with interpersonal relationships. The golden mean is the art of getting the degree and timing just right to achieve a balance between any two extremes. In terms of management one should stress limits, neither sticking rigidly to rules and regulations, nor changing them willy-nilly. Many people believe the Chinese do not work according to principles but adopt an ad hoc approach in dealing with almost everything. But in fact, the Chinese do have a principle: it is the 'doctrine of the mean'.

Currently, world management models are divided by some into three types - Western, Japanese and Chinese. The Western management model emphasizes the importance of rules and regulations, management organization and structure; relatively less attention is given to human feelings. Japanese-style management is mainly concerned with conformity, teamwork spirit, loyalty and cooperation. By contrast the Chinese style in business management is to stress the integration and synergy of the individual with the whole organisation. While emphasising the importance of systematization and nationality it also pays great attention to shared values, harmonious inter-personal relations and excellent team spirit. It can be said that Chinese-style management takes law as its structure, rationality as its core and feelings as its inspiration.

Different models of business management can learn from each other, utilizing the strengths of others to compensate for one's own deficiencies. With the development of economic globalization, Eastern and Western management cultures are displaying a tendency to converge. Management in the future will place greater emphasis on human values and become more inclusive.

Lao Zi and Human Resource Development and Management

Laozi's family name was Li, and his full name was Li Er. He lived approximately between 571 and 471 BC. His works include the Lao Zi, also known as the Dao de jing, (Classic of the Way and the Power). The Dao de jing was later regarded as a work on the arts of leadership and management. The doctrines propounded by Laozi are especially relevant in the present day to the development and management of human resources in business.

According to Laozi, the prerequisite for human resource management is to understand people; only by understanding a person can you employ them intelligently. Yet how should we go about understanding a person? How should we assess a person's capabilities and worth? Laozi believes that those who manage others should first of all be wise, should "know thyself". They should be unbiased, not give credence to slander, not be jealous of the talents of others, and not be corrupt and accept bribes. Only those with such qualities can ensure that genuinely talented people are employed in key posts.

On the issue of what talent is, Laozi believes that there are no useless people in the world. In other words, a competent manager should be good at discovering the strengths of every employee, using their good points and avoiding their weaknesses in order to ensure they work for the benefit of the organization. Leaders should not seek perfection in people, because there are no perfect people in the world. Nor is there anyone in the world who is useless: there are only people whose talents have not yet been discovered and people who do not know how to employ others. In recognising outstanding talent, leaders must be good at identifying the basic character below the surface, and not be taken in by the superficial appearance of things. If judgment is made based solely upon appearance without due regard to the nature and potential of a person, truly outstanding talents may be wasted. Leaders should also understand that those who are good at showing off may not necessarily have real talent and knowledge. Therefore, they should value and promote those employees who are committed and work hard.

The purpose of identifying talented people is to make use of them. How to use appropriately the potential of talented people is extremely important. Laozi believes that leaders should be good at delegating power. Since the best leaders have the ability to motivate their subordinates to use their own initiative, the latter are often unaware of their leader's presence. Once a job is done, the subordinates will all think " I did this". Of course, good leaders should be at the centre of the power as well; this is mainly manifested in making prompt decisions on major policy issues. However, leaders do not need constantly to concern themselves with the process of implementing a decision. Instead, they should motivate their subordinates to develop fully their sense of initiative at work and give them the opportunity to utilize their abilities.

Leaders should be clear in giving instructions to subordinates. We all know that things are dynamic, but at a particular time and in a certain place they are also comparatively static. In Laozi's mind, "change" is an exceptionally important concept. However, Laozi also emphasized that the leaders should not constantly change their instructions, leaving their subordinates at a loss on what to do. Leaders should "remain steadfast in the face of change", enabling their subordinates to know what path to follow during a time of change, and so achieve the agreed targets.

Tian Ji and the Horse Race

Tian Ji, a great general of the State of Qi, loved horse racing. Once, he held a competition with King Wei of Qi. They each agreed to divide their horses into three categories: superior, medium and inferior. During the competition the superior horses would race each other, then the medium horses and finally the inferior horses. As King Wei's horses were much better than Tian Ji's in every category, after a few races Tian Ji had lost every time.

Tian Ji felt very disappointed. He was about to leave the racecourse before the competition was over when his good friend Sun Bin called him over. Patting him on the shoulder Sun Bin said, "I was watching the races; the King's horses are not much faster than yours." Before Sun Bin could even finish his sentence, Tian Ji glared at him, "I never thought even you would be mocking me!" Sun Bin replied: "I am not mocking you. I am asking you to race him one more time. I have a way I'm sure will enable you to beat him." Tian Ji looked doubtfully at Sun Bin, "Are you suggesting I change horses?" Sun Bin shook his head, saying, "There is no need to replace a single horse." Tian Ji was not convinced, "Wouldn't that mean I'll lose again?" Sun Bin assured him confidently, "You just do as I say."

King Wei of Qi had won every race in the competition so far. He was smugly lauding the abilities of his horses when he saw Tian Ji and Sun Bin coming over. So he stood up and said to them, "What's this, are you still not giving up?" Tian Ji replied, "Of course I'm not giving up. Let's have another race!" With a thunderous crash, he emptied a great pile of silver coins onto the table as his stake in the race. Seeing this, King Wei immediately told his retainers to fetch all the silver he had won from the previous races, and on top of that he also added a thousand taels of gold; this was all placed on the table. King Wei then said, "Well then, let us begin!"

The competition began again. Sun Bin first raced an inferior horse against King Wei's superior horse and lost the first round. King Wei stood up and said: "It's hard to believe the illustrious Master Sun could come up with such a bad strategy." Sun Bin ignored him. Then began the second round. Sun Bin chose a superior horse to race against the King's medium horse and won this round. The King became a bit worried. In the third round Sun Bin chose a medium horse to race the King's inferior horse, and was once again victorious. This time, the King was dumbfounded. The result of the competition was two wins out of three, so of course Tian Ji beat King Wei. Despite the fact that these were the same horses, through a simple change in the running order he succeeded in turning defeat into victory.

Business Practices - Customs and Etiquettes

Chinese people pay special attention to the others' social status and title when interacting with people. Normally they would address each other using the title of their position, for example "Manager Zhao", "Factory Director Li", "General Manager Xie", etc. to indicate respect for the person they are addressing. This is even true for those who are retired. People still politely address them using the title of their former position. This is because Chinese do not forget the past. Nowadays the title "Teacher" is not only used to address those who teach, but also those who are older, more experienced and more knowledgeable.

Before going to China one should not only read background information on the client, but also some general information on China. It is even better if one can learn to speak a few sentences in Chinese. Greeting your hosts in Chinese leaves a good impression as it demonstrates your respect for and appreciation of their language. When presenting a business card, one should use both hands. Upon receiving a card, one should take a brief look at it before putting it away. The Chinese people like the colour red, not black or white. Therefore attention should be given to this when it comes to attire and the packaging of gifts. The gift should not be too expensive, as that could cause a suspicion of bribery, nor should it be too cheap, as that would indicate a lack of respect for the host. It is best to give something like an arts and crafts object, moderate in price and characteristic of Western culture. The Chinese word for "clock" sounds the same as the word for "end". Therefore do not give clocks as gifts to the Chinese, nor umbrellas or anything sharp. Lucky numbers for the Chinese are 8 and 6, and the most unlucky number is 4.

Topics of conversation are also very important. The success or failure of a business negotiation can depend greatly upon the conversation you and your host have over dinner and how the Chinese host perceives you. Due to the great divergence in views between the West and China, subjects such as Taiwan, Tibet, the Falungong and human rights are better avoided. During meals the Chinese like to toast their guests and help them by filling their glasses and plates. The Chinese like to savour the taste of delicious food, thus they have the habit of making sounds when they eat. They also often make a slurping sound when drinking soup, which can be quite hard for Westerners to accept. Similarly there are some Western habits that Chinese find hard to accept too, such as blowing one's nose very loudly, licking the fingers and biting one's nails. When inviting Chinese people out for meals in return, it is best to avoid offering them Western food. Also it is best in the evening, as they tend to have a siesta at midday. What is more, you should offer to others when smoking or having snack rather than just looking after yourself.

Chinese respect the elderly and enjoy helping others. If they appear to be too fussy towards you, it is because they respect you. The Chinese tend to be indirect when speaking, and like to use words such as "perhaps" and "maybe". This is because they are very concerned with 'face' and do not want to reject you outright, therefore you should save their face too. So do not use harsh languages when negotiating, respect the other party and refrain from making rash judgments. If you cause embarrassment to the host or guest, even a momentary blunder, it is always likely to bring a severe loss of business.

Business Practices - Interpersonal Relationships

Due to cultural differences, even the most modern Western management practices may fail when transferred to China. A good strategy for cross cultural management is communication and exchange. Western investors discover that it is not an easy task to find appropriate co-investors or managers in China that satisfy their standards. They suspect the Chinese party may not fully understand Western business practices, whilst the Chinese party may find them too high-handed and unwilling to listen to suggestions made by the Chinese.

Western management practices tend to follow the principle that: "work is work and personal relationships are something else". But for Chinese, these two may be combined. Western criticism is directed at the matter, not the person; the Chinese however will generally direct first at the person and then at the matter. Westerners prefer to be direct when exchanging opinions. If an interpersonal conflict arises in business management, they prefer to explain the real situation by setting out a vast quantity of facts, and to use very direct language. However, the Chinese believe such an approach leads to loss of face and hence prefer a more implicit way that saves face for those concerned. Chinese employees expect companies to provide "social welfare", such as shuttle buses for getting to and fro work, and weekend leisure activities etc. Westerners tend not to get involved in anything outside work, thus leaving private space for individuals. Westerners see it as problematic when policies lack transparency, while Chinese do not see this as a serious problem. Chinese employees are used to solving problems by reducing them from big to small, and eventually to nothing at all, yet a Western manager wants to know as soon as there is a problem so it can be solved straight away. Chinese people tend to appeal to authority and precedent, while Westerners place greater importance on innovation in management. Westerners like to see results while Chinese like to build up networks of contacts. Western employees may ask directly for a pay rise, but Chinese generally would not behave like that. Chinese tend to be rather passive, and like to wait for others to recognise their worth. Most Chinese staff, especially technical staff, tend to belong to the "nose to the grindstone" type, hoping to have their merit recognised by their seniors, but ignorant of how to protect their rights and lacking awareness of how to conduct modern business negotiations. One thing Chinese staff would not tolerate is any form of degrading corporal punishment. According to Confucian tradition parents and seniors could use corporal punishment against young people, but now Chinese have already rejected this aspect of Confucianism. Especially after many years of Communist Party management and education, the concept of equality is now deeply ingrained in people's hearts. Corporal punishment of staff would destroy the reputation of an enterprise and make the business collapse.

Simply put, it is characteristic of Chinese employees to have a rather dependent personality and to be relatively introverted; they will strive for harmony and not directly clash with superiors, nor will they upset others. However, they have a strong sense of fairness, and although they may appear muddled, in fact they are very clear in their minds. They also place great importance on personal improvement, frugality, family life and personal health, and they refrain from excessive drinking, late nights and wild entertainment.

Case Study I – A Multinational Company's Setback in China

The formula used by a certain U.S electrical appliance company as its business strategy was as follows. First of all, to gain a foothold in a country by forming a joint venture with a leading company in that country, and then to build up its own market position, and to take management control of the joint venture in the shortest time possible, with everything from production and administration to sales, all in the hands of the U.S. party. At the same time, they sought to rapidly establish their own sales network and related operating systems, avoiding the sales channels of the co-investor, by creating their own network to give themselves sufficient technology and market advantages so as not be restrained by their co-investor in future market operations.

This is a very logical business model, but why didn't it work in China?

To begin with, before establishing the joint venture with the Chinese enterprise, the company entrusted the task of making advertisements to an "international advertising agency" that did not fully understand the Chinese market. The advertisements were not sufficiently forceful, with the result that the U.S. brand name lacked consumer recognition.

Secondly, the company set up a complete U.S. style management structure as soon as the venture was established. Cost controls were lax at a time when the business was weak, with the cost of just four American managers alone amounting to US$800,000 a year. In addition, as the company was in a rush to establish its own sales network, management costs rose exponentially, eventually exceeding what the joint venture itself could sustain.

Thirdly, the company insisted on importing from the US the chemical raw materials used for manufacturing refrigerators, increasing the costs by over 1/3. Employee management was also ineffective: morale was low, which directly affected production. This all led to excessive production costs for the company. Additionally being used to normal rules and practice, the U.S. management did not have any idea of what "triangular debt chains" were. As a result many payments were not received on time, creating cash flow problems for the company. Fourthly, the company recruited professional managers from overseas and placed them directly into the management ranks of the joint venture. Due to their unfamiliarity with China and its market, they could only rely on management approaches commonly used in other countries. Consequently there were many ill-suited business strategies, leading to business setbacks. For example in the management of the joint venture producing microwaves, the company followed old procedures and sent its market promotion strategy first to the Hong Kong branch and then to the U.S. headquarters for approval. This took two to three months. By the time the strategy was approved the market opportunity had long been lost.

As the company was not familiar with Chinese market, it simply persisted in cloning so-called "mature management models", and in the end it was squeezed out of the market. This case proved that although the party with the majority of the shares can exert more control, the recipe for success in the case of multi- nationals managing joint ventures is to fully utilise the experience of the local partner.

Case Study II – Coca Cola's Success in China

The world's largest soft drink maker Coca Cola entered China in 1979. Since then it has established 28 bottling plants, with a total investment of over US$1.1 billion. China has become the sixth largest market for Coca Cola after the U.S., Mexico, Germany, Brazil and Japan.

Coca Cola implements globally its market strategy of "thinking locally and operating locally", utilising local perspectives and integrating itself into the local environment. This approach has strongly pushed forward marketing and sales. In the year 2000, Coca Cola moved its regional headquarters from Hong Kong to Shanghai, and 98% of the raw materials were procured locally. In 2002, for the first time it appointed three local Chinese as vice presidents. In order to better adapt to the competitive demands of the Chinese market, Coca Cola formally began using its new Chinese logo on the 18th February 2003.

Coca Cola was one of the first companies to create TV commercials locally. The company specified that the commercials should reflect the attitudes of the local people. During the 2001 Spring Festival, a special "A Fu" New Year packaging was introduced, utilising the local New Year good luck image to reach out to consumers. This was Coca Cola's third "Lunar New Year Advertisement", which along with the "Great Windmill" and "Dancing Dragon" was specifically designed for the Chinese market. The two children depicted on the Coca Cola packaging were the familiar "A Fu" clay dolls, both holding Coca Cola bottles and wreathed in smiles. The background colour was mainly red, with some bright yellow. The red primarily represented Coca Cola whilst the bright yellow primarily represented China. The appearance of the very Chinese image of the "A Fu" dolls struck a chord with the public who mentally identified with Coca Cola's new packaging. Through festive celebrations such as putting up couplets and letting off fireworks, the company's commercial created the feeling that Coca Cola was also celebrating the Spring Festival along with everyone. During the days when the Chinese were with their families, Coca Cola used a family setting to promote its 2.25-litre Coca Cola. The image of good fortune for the whole family subtly indicated the product's target customers, and 2.25-litre bottles were well suited to the consumption levels when families entertain guests. Thus this commercial indicates that since entering the Chinese market twenty years ago, Coca Cola has now become part of the lives of Chinese people. Furthermore a Sinified Coca Cola is definitely guaranteed better sales in China. Coca Cola also released a special set of ring-pull cans with twelve Chinese zodiac animals, said to be the first set of commemorative memorabilia in the world focused exclusively on China. Its popularity was such that people from Hong Kong shipped crates of it back home from Beijing.

Coca Cola was well aware that it was not enough just to win over the stomachs of Chinese customers, they had to win over their hearts as well. Therefore Coca Cola actively participated in a whole range of welfare activities, building Project Hope primary schools and libraries in the countryside and funding athletic events for teenagers in cities. Within 30 minutes of the news of China's successful bid for the Olympics, 30,000 cases of specially designed Olympic gold cans came off the production line at the Beijing Coca Cola Co Ltd and were transported overnight to all major shopping malls and retailers.

Brief Introduction to the Haier Group

The Haier Group was founded in 1984. For the past twenty years it has steadily grown and become a large trans-national corporation fairly well known both at home and abroad. Its product lines began with just refrigerators in 1984 but now cover over 15,100 products in 96 major categories including home appliances, home entertainment and computer products. These products are now exported to over 160 countries and regions. In 2004 Haier's revenue exceeded 100 billion RMB.

Haier has established a globally competitive network in design, procurement, manufacturing, marketing and servicing. The company has 10 industrial parks, 30 overseas plants and production bases, eight overseas design centres and 58,800 retail outlets. In China, Haier holds 21% of the entire domestic electric appliance market, with a 34% share in the home white goods sector, which is beyond the international benchmark for monopolies. In the small home appliance market, Haier has a market share of 14%, beating established famous brands to become the leading producer. Internationally, Haier small refrigerators and drinks cabinets have taken a leading share of the US market; its washing machines dominate the Iranian market, and its air conditioners rank the first in terms of market share in Cyprus.

Based on its practical experience, Haier has created an "OEC" management model with unique Chinese characteristics. "O" stands for Omni-bearing and all roundness, "E" for everyone, everyday and everything; and "C" for control and management. Its main idea can be summed up as: within the whole company, everyone deals successfully with every task, everyday.

From August 1998, Haier began piloting its management model of the quality market chain, abbreviated as the SST system, which is an upgrade and improvement of the OCE. SST is derived from the first letter of the phonetic pinyin for three Chinese words: Reward, Claim and Trip. Reward is to receive remuneration through service; claim means that compensation is necessary if the contract between departments is not fulfilled; and trip refers to the time when neither reward nor claim is involved, the third party will automatically "trip". The SST system has incorporated every process in production and every employee into the entire market control structure. At the same time, the income of every employee reflects market performance. This practice has greatly motivated the staff and raised their potential, improving the overall standard and vitality of the whole company. Haier's management approach fully demonstrates a management philosophy based upon the concept of putting people first.

The Yiwu International Commodities Fair, China

The Yiwu International Commodities Fair (abbreviated to the Yiwu Fair) is the only international fair of daily consumer commodities in China approved by the Chinese State Council. The Yiwu Fair was first established in 1995 and so far 9 fairs have taken place. It is now the largest, most influential and effective fair for small commodities in China.

Yiwu, known as China's Small Commodities City, is located in Zhejiang Province. Yiwu currently has a business area of over 1 million square meters, with about 40,000 stall places dealing with over 200,000 kinds of small commodities in 28 major categories, effectively covering almost every type of daily consumable. The city is the biggest hub for distribution, information and exhibition of small commodities, as well as the largest export base for small commodities in China.

The Yiwu Exhibition Centre is designed to accommodate a full range of exhibition requirements. Exhibition vehicles can enter each exhibition hall directly. There are 8 escalators leading from the entrances which are conveniently located to provide access for visitors. All stands are equipped with international direct dial phones and internet access, and thus are e-commerce friendly with the world at your finger tips and on the screen.

In 2004, the Yiwu Fair had over 70,000 square metres of exhibition floor space, with 3,000 international standard booths. A total of 1,790 firms from over 20 countries, and 26 Chinese provinces and municipalities exhibited at the Fair, with about 20% of firms coming from abroad. Over 30% of the exhibited products were brand names from well established companies. Deals worth of 7.43 billion RMB were agreed during the fair, of which US$563 million was export-related, making up 62.9% of the total trading at the Fair.

The 2004 Yiwu Fair had seven exhibition halls. Hall A and Hall E were for craftwork; Hall B was for leather products, cases and bags, and cosmetics; Hall C and Hall D were for top-end products; Hall E was for electronic and electrical appliances, garments and knitware; and Hall G was dedicated to household utensils, sports articles, hardware, and toys. The 2004 Yiwu Fair also set up an e-business area for the first time. A total of 23 domestic and foreign online companies including alibaba.com and Google exhibited at the Fair.

Foreign visitors attending the 2004 Yiwu Fair came from 164 countries and regions around the world, of which 62% were from Asia, 13% from Europe, 14% from America, 7% from Africa and 2% from Oceania, with the remaining 2% from the other regions of the world.

More details of the Yiwu International Fair can be found on its website at http://www.chinafairs.org/index.htm .

The future of the Chinese Economy

The world has entered an era of globalisation since the 1990s, accompanied by the rapid development of science and technology, the increasingly internationalised division of labour and an intensification of the internationalisation of production and capital. Relations between the global economies have become closer than ever before.

During the past few years, China has been one of the fastest growing economies in the world. China's rapid economic growth has attracted a lot of FDI as well as many trans-national corporations into the Chinese market. After her ascension to the WTO, China has removed many restrictions on foreign mergers and acquisitions. The government supports and encourages its state owned companies to restructure, and actively guides mergers and acquisitions involving state owned national enterprises. The intention has been to keep 80 to 100 state-owned companies under direct contral of the central government engaged in vital and strategic industries such as resources, energy, metallurgy, and automobiles. The government plans to foster and develop just 30 to 50 large companies or conglomerates that are globally competitive out of the current total of 179 state-owned national enterprises.

Internationally, China is one of the major sources of economic growth for most Asian countries. What ever the product, there is always a market in China - industrial products from Japan and South Korea, agricultural products from Vietnam and India, livestock from Australia and New Zealand, oil from central Asian, minerals from South Asia and all kinds of raw materials from ASEAN. Meanwhile, China provides these countries with huge commercial opportunities, attracting much of the idle capital from the Asia Pacific region to invest in China. China's influence has also reached outside Asia. Brazil and Argentina are amongst the many countries whose business dealings with China have increased 4 to 6 fold. China's rise is not only on a regional scale in Asia, but on a global scale in the world.

It is by no means an easy task for the Chinese economy to have achieved such results. Some unstable and unhealthy factors have emerged in the process of China's rapid growth since 2004. The amount of land available for cultivation has been decreasing yearly, and investment in fixed asset has risen to the point of overheating. At the same time there is a growing shortage of coal, electricity and oil. At this important crossroads in China's economic development, the Chinese government has decided to take macro economic control and make adjustment accordingly to deal with these problems. After just over a year, as the current situation attests, government policies have contributed greatly to the stable development of the national economy without slowing down economic growth. During this period, the Chinese government has taken a down to earth approach with extra care given to the extent, timing and intervals in the macro economic control and adjustment. The flexibility with which China has used the economic measures to achieve this demonstrates that the Chinese government is becoming more experienced in guiding the country's economy.

The Chinese economy will continue to face difficult problems and challenges during its development. However, as long as the Chinese government exerts rational control and makes adjustments accordingly, and ensures that the relevant policies are implemented, China's economy will continue to grow steadily and rapidly.

词汇表

阿福	Āfú	专名	New Year good luck figurine of young boy	17
阿喜	Āxǐ	专名	New Year good luck figurine of young girl	17
阿根廷	Āgēntíng	专名	Argentina	20
阿里巴巴	Ālǐbābā	专名	an online B2B website (http://china.alibaba.com)	19
暗示	ànshì	动/名	imply, hint	17
澳大利亚	Àodàlìyà	专名	Australia	20
熬夜	áoyè	动	stay up late into the night	15
叭哒	bādā	象声	smack lips, sound made when eating	14
巴西	Bāxī	专名	Braizil	17
把握	bǎwò	动	grasp, seize	20
霸道	bàdào	形	overbearing, high-handed	17
包容性	bāoróngxìng	名	tolerance	11
宝洁	Bǎojié	专名	Procter & Gamble	17
本质	běnzhì	名	(basic) nature	12
比比皆是	bǐbǐjiēshì	形	abundant; everywhere	11
避实击虚	bìshíjīxū	动	avoid the strong and attack the weak	13
编制	biānzhì	动	compile	18
贬低	biǎndī	动	debase, belittle	14
标识	biāoshí	名	mark, sign	17
摒弃	bìngqì	动	discard, give up	15
剥	bō	动	peel off, throw off	17
播种面积	bōzhòngmiànji	名	area of cultivation	20
波动	bōdòng	动/名	be volatile, volatility	20
博览会	bólǎnhuì	名	expo	19
伯乐	Bólè	专名	name of famous horse expert	15
参展商	cānzhǎnshāng	名	exhibitor	19
蝉联	chánlián	动	retain, be awarded on successive occasions	18
谗言	chányán	名	slander, malicious talk	12
长袍	chángpáo	名	long gown (traditional scholar's garment)	17
成交额	chéngjiāo'é	名	volume of business	19
承受力	chéngshòulì	名	ability to bear	16
诚意	chéngyì	名	sincerity	16
重组	chóngzǔ	动/名	restructure, restructuring	20
春联	chūnlián	名	Spring Festival couplet	17
凑合	còuhe	动	make do, put up with	14

错位竞争	cuòwèijìngzhēng	动	skewed competition	13
大发雷霆	dàfāléitíng	动	fly into a rage, lose one's temper	15
大惑不解	dàhuòbùjiě	形	be extremely puzzled	15
大洋洲	dàyángzhōu	专名	Oceania	19
当机立断	dāngjīlìduàn	动	be decisive, make immediate decision	12
道德伦理	dàodélúnlǐ	名	ethics and morality	11
导致	dǎozhì	动	lead to	11
得意洋洋	déyìyángyáng	形/副	conceited	13
得益于	déyìyú	动	benefit from	12
得罪	dézuì	动	offend	15
登陆	dēnglù	动	to land, to get into a market	16
电子商务	diànzǐshāngwù	名	e-business	19
顶撞	dǐngzhuàng	动	contradict, clash with	15
丢卒保车	diūzúbǎojū	动	lose a soldier to save the chariot, sacrifice a minor thing to save the major one	13
东道国	dōngdàoguó	名	host country	16
东风汽车股份有限公司	Dōngfēngqìchē gǔfènyǒuxiàngōngsī	专名	Dongfeng Automobile Co. Ltd	18
斗室	dǒushì	名	small room or dwelling	17
赌注	dǔzhù	名	(gambling) stake	13
独特	dútè	形	distinctive, unique	12
法轮功	Fǎlúngōng	名	Falungong	14
凡事	fánshì	名	everything	11
非同小可	fēitóngxiǎokě	形	no small matter	17
废人	fèirén	名	useless people	12
分寸	fēncùn	名	appropriate degree	11
氛围	fēnwéi	名	atmosphere	11
份额	fèn'é	名	(market) share	18
丰田	Fēngtián	专名	Toyota	17
奉献	fèngxìan	动/名	contribution, devote to	11
福利待遇	fúlìdàiyù	名	social benefits, welfare benefits	18
服气	fúqì	动	admit defeat, concede	13
服饰	fúshì	名	clothing	14
概括	gàikuò	动	summarise, epitomise	18
概念	gàiniàn	名	concept	12
高尚	gāoshàng	形	revered	14
恭恭敬敬	gōnggōngjìngjìng	副	respectfully	14
功能齐全	gōngnéngqíquán	名	complete functionality, fully equipped	19
公益	gōngyì	名	for the benefit of public	17
共鸣	gòngmíng	名	resonance, sympathetic response	17

谷歌	Gǔgē	专名	Google	19
顾及	gùjí	动	take into account, consider	14
雇员	gùyuán	名	employee	12
观察	guānchá	名/动	observe, observation	11
贯穿于	guànchuānyú	动	run through, permeate	13
光辉灿烂	guānghuīcànlàn	形	splendid, brilliant	11
规矩	guīju	名	rules and regulations	14
规章	guīzhāng	名	regulation, rule	11
哈佛大学	Háfódàxué	专名	Harvard University	18
海尔	Haǐ'ěr	专名	Haier, a major home appliance producer	18
含蓄	hánxù	形	indirect, implicit	15
合二为一	héèrwéiyī	动	combine two into one	15
和谐	héxié	名/形	harmony, harmonious	11
赫赫有名	hèhèyǒumíng	形	illustrious, very famous	13
贺岁	hèsuì	名	celebration of the New Year	17
接轨	jiēguǐ	动	come into line with	18
后发制人	hòufāzhìrén	动	win through counter-attacking strategy	13
画面	huàmiàn	名	picture, scene	17
环节	huánjié	名	link	14
缓解	huǎnjiě	名	reduce, mitigate	20
唤起	huànqǐ	动	raise, awake, kindle	17
汇集	huìjí	动	assemble, bring together	19
火候	huǒhou	名	timing	11
激发	jīfā	动	stimulate	18
积极性	jījíxìng	名	initiative; enthusiasm	12
吉祥	jíxiáng	形	auspicious, lucky	17
既定	jìdìng	形	predetermined	12
嫉妒	jìdù	动/名	envy, be jealous of	12
计谋	jìmóu	名	stratagem	13
纪念品	jìniànpǐn	名	souvenir	17
夹菜	jiācài	动	pick up food with chopsticks	14
家居用品	jiājūyòngpǐn	名	household goods	19
夹杂	jiāzá	动	mixed with	17
驾驭	jiàyù	动	control	20
见解	jiànjiě	名	view, understanding	11
讲究	jiǎngjiu	动	be particularly about	11
届	jiè	量	Measure for events, meetings, etc.	19
节奏	jiézòu	名	rhythm	20
借鉴	jièjiàn	动	draw on the experience of	11
紧凑	jǐncòu	形	busy, full (schedule)	16
紧攀其上	jǐnpānqíshàng	动	firmly attached to it	17

经济合作与发展组织	Jīngjìhézuò yǔfāzhǎngzǔzhī	专名	OECD (Organisation for Economic Cooperation and Development)	20
精辟	jīngpì	形	brilliant, penetrating	11
精品	jīngpǐn	名	luxury goods	19
竟然	jìngrán	副	unexpectedly	13
静止	jìngzhǐ	形	static	12
军事家	jūnshìjiā	名	military strategist	13
克隆	kèlóng	动	clone; copy	16
恐惧	kǒngjù	名	fear	17
控股	kònggǔ	动/名	have controlling share	16
夸耀	kuāyào	动	brag about, show off	13
快捷	kuàijié	形	speedy, swift	19
矿藏	kuàngcáng	名	mineral resources	20
框架	kuàngjià	名	framework	11
理念	lǐniàn	名	concept; belief	11
礼仪	lǐyí	名	ritual	14
利器	lìqì	名	sharp object, weapon	14
立邦	Lìbāng	专名	Nippon	17
廉价	liánjià	形	low cost; cheap	20
灵魂	línghún	名	soul	11
灵活多样	línghuóduōyàng	形	flexible and varied	19
垄断	lǒngduàn	名/动	monopoly, monopolise	18
屡…屡…	lǚ….lǚ…	副	repeatedly	13
履约	lǚyuē	动	fulfil contract	18
落实执行	luòshízhíxíng	动	implementation	20
埋没	máimò	动	neglect; bury	12
埋头苦干	máitóukǔgàn	动	devote oneself to work, work hard	12
卖弄	màinong	动	show-off	12
迷惑	míhuò	动/名	mislead; confusion	12
民族企业	mínzúqǐyè	名	national industry	20
明智	míngzhì	形	sensible, wise	12
墨西哥	Mòxīgē	专名	Mexico	17
木偶	mù'ǒu	名	puppet, doll	17
目瞪口呆	mùdèngkǒudāi	形	dumbstruck, stupefied	13
耐克	Nàikè	专名	Nike	17
难堪	nánkān	形	embarrassed	14
囊括	nángkuò	动	include, embrace	19
内向	nèixiàng	名	introverted personality	15
浓缩于	nóngsuōyú	动	condense to, shrink to	19
派生	pàishēng	动	derive	14

庞大	pángdà	形	enormous	20
泡沫经济	pàomòjīngjì	名	bubble economy	20
培育	péiyù	动/名	nurture, foster	20
培植	péizhí	动/名	cultivate, nurture	16
偏重于	piānzhòngyú	动	lay emphasis on, stress	11
皮具	píjù	名	leather products,	19
频频	pínpín	副	frequently	12
聘请	pìnqǐng	动/名	recruit, recruitment	16
平稳	píngwěn	形	smooth and steady	20
齐全	qíquán	形	complete	19
恰到好处	qiàdàohǎochù	形/副	just right, perfect	11
洽谈会	qiàtánhuì	名	fair	19
迁	qiān	动	move	17
谦虚	qiānxū	形/名	modest	11
前提	qiántí	名	premise, prerequisite	12
强势品牌	qiángshìpǐnpái	名	leading brand	18
青岛啤酒股份有限公司	Qīngdǎopíjiǔ gǔfènyǒuxiàngōngsī	专名	Tsingtao Brewery Company Limited	18
倾向于	qīngxiàngyú	动	tend to	15
趋同倾向	qūtóngqīngxiàng	名	tendency towards convergence	11
取长补短	qǔchángbǔduǎn	动	learn from others' strengths to make up one's own deficiencies	11
取代	qǔdài	动/名	replace	20
权威	quānwēi	名	authority	17
日用五金	rìyòngwǔjīn	名	everyday hardware goods	19
仁	rén	名	benevolence	11
人力资源	rénlìzīyuán	名	human resources	12
人心涣散	rénxīnhuànsàn	动	no shared sense of belonging	16
认可	rènkě	名	recognition, approval	16
任命	rènmìng	名/动	appointment; appoint	12
融合	rónghé	名/动	integrate, integration	11
入乡随俗	rùxiāngsuísú	动	follow local customs	14
瑞士洛桑国际管理学院	Ruìshìluòsāngguójì guǎnlǐxuéyuàn	专名	Swiss Lausanne international management institute	18
塞浦路斯	Sàipǔlùsī	专名	Cyprus	18
三角债	sānjiǎozhài	名	debt involving three parties	16
扫兴	sǎoxìng	名/动	feel dejected	13
色彩黯淡	sècǎi'àndàn	形	with dark and dull colours	17
商检	shāngjiǎn	名	commodity inspection	19
赏罚分明	shǎngfáfēnmíng	动	be fair in rewards and punishment	12
上策	shàngcè	名	best strategy	16

上乘	shàngchèng	形	top grade, high end	16
上海大众汽车有限公司	Shànghǎidàzhòng qìchēyǒuxiàngōngsī	专名	Shanghai Volkswagen Co. Ltd	18
上述	shàngshù	形	above-mentioned	20
申奥	shēn'ào	名	bid to host Olympic Games	17
深入人心	shēnrùrénxīn	动	reach the hearts of the people	15
渗透	shèntòu	动	permeate	11
施展	shīzhǎn	动	demonstrate, utilize	12
失衡	shīhéng	动/名	imbalance	20
实践	shíjiàn	动/名	practice	15
实事求是	shíshìqiúshì	名	seek truth from facts, practical and realistic	20
实属不易	shíshǔbúyì	形	really difficult, truly impressive	20
十全十美	shíquánshíměi	形	perfect	12
始终	shǐzhōng	副	from beginning to end, always	13
市场链	shìchǎngliàn	名	market chain	18
适得其反	shìdéqífǎn	动	run counter to one's desire	17
受挫	shòucuò	动	suffer from setback	16
甩手不管	shuǎishǒubùguǎn	动	wash one's hand of	15
疏忽	shūhū	形	neglect, overlook	14
属下	shǔxià	名	subordinate	12
顺序	shùnxù	名	order	13
思维	sīwéi	名	way of thinking	11
松散	sōngsǎn	形	slack, sparse (schedule)	16
随从	suícóng	名	entourage	13
索赔	suǒpéi	动	compensation seeking	18
索酬	suǒchóu	动	reward seeking	18
所谓	suǒwèi	形	so-called	11
诉诸	sùzhù	动	resort to	15
贪公受贿	tāngōngshòuhuì	动	greedy and corrupt	12
套用	tàoyòng	动	indiscriminately adopt	16
特殊	tèshū	名/形	special	15
提拔	tíbá	动/名	promote	12
体罚	tǐfá	名/动	corporal punishment	15
通用汽车	tōngyòngqìchē	专名	General Motors	17
投标	tóubiāo	动/名	put in a bid	15
头衔	tóuxián	名	title (of a person)	14
挖苦	wākǔ	动/名	mock, ridicule	13
婉转	wǎnzhuǎn	形	indirect	14
妄加评判	wàngjiāpíngpàn	动	make unwarranted criticism	14
为人处事	wéirénchǔshì	动	dealings with others	11

文体用品	wéntǐyòngpǐn	名	cultural and sports goods	19
委托	wěituō	动/名	commission (sb to do sth)	16
未必	wèibì	副	not necessarily	12
侮辱人格	wūrǔréngé	动	insult one's integrity	15
无所适从	wúsuǒshìcóng	副	be at a loss as to what to do	12
武断	wǔduàn	形	arbitrary, autocratic	15
午觉	wǔjiào	名	afternoon nap	14
狭隘	xiá'ài	形	narrow	16
下意识	xiàyìshi	副	subconsciously	12
下载	xiàzǎi	动	download	19
贤才	xiáncái	名	virtuous and talented people	12
娴熟	xiánshú	形	skilled, adept	20
嫌疑	xiányí	名/动	suspicion, suspect	14
闲置资本	xiánzhìzīběn	名	idle capital	20
箱包	xiāngbāo	名	cases and bags	19
相让	xiāngràng	动	offer to others	14
象征	xiàngzhēng	名	symbol	17
现象	xiànxiàng	名	(external) appearance; phenomenon	12
消耗量	xiāohàoliàng	名	consumption amount	17
笑容可掬	xiàoróngkějū	形	wreathed in smiles, beaming	17
携带	xiédài	名/动	carry, take	19
协调	xiétiáo	名/动	harmonization; co-ordinate	11
擤鼻涕	xǐngbíti	动	blow one's nose	14
心慌意乱	xīnhuāngyìluàn	形	agitated	13
欣赏	xīnshǎng	动	appreciate, show appreciation for	14
新西兰	Xīnxīlán	专名	New Zealand	20
胸有成竹	xiōngyǒuchéngzhú	副/形	knowingly; confident in ones plans	13
酗酒	xùjiǔ	动/名	drink excessively	15
样品	yàngpǐn	名	sample product	16
咬	yǎo	动	bite, chew	14
冶金	yějīn	名	metallurgy	20
依附性	yīfùxìng	名	anaclisis	15
依赖	yīlài	名	dependence	20
伊朗	Yīlǎng	专名	Iran	18
疑惑	yíhuò	副/动	doubtfully, be doubtful	13
一贯	yíguàn	副	uniform, unchanging	16
一味	yíwèi	副	blindly, invariably	16
一致性	yízhìxìng	名	consistency	11
一时疏忽	yìshíshūhū	副	a single oversight, a careless moment	14
一体化	yìtǐhuà	名	unification, integration	11
以人为本	yǐrénwéiběn	动	put people first	11

以和为贵	yǐhéwéiguì	动	regard harmony as the most important thing	11
以身作则	yǐshēnzuòzé	动	set an example oneself	12
易拉罐	yìlāguàn	名	easy open can (for drinks)	17
义乌	Yìwū	专名	city in Zhejiang province	19
饮食业	yǐnshíyè	动/名	food and drink industry	18
印度	Yìndù	专名	India	20
荧屏	yíngpíng	名	monitor, screen (computer)	19
营销网点	yíngxiāowǎngdiǎn	名	point of sale (in a network)	18
遇事化小	yùshìhuàxiǎo	动	minimise problems	15
源泉	yuánquán	名	source	20
咂	zā	动	lick, suck	14
赞助	zànzhù	名/动	sponsor	17
造就	zàojiù	动/名	achieve; train	12
增设	zēngshè	动	install in addition to	19
扎根于	zhāgēnyú	动	be rooted in	12
掌管	zhǎngguǎn	动/名	take charge of, control	16
招待	zhāodài	动/名	treat, receive	16
招聘	zhāopìn	动	recruit	18
照搬	zhàobān	动/名	copy, follow slavishly	15
真才实学	zhēncáishíxué	名	real ability and learning	12
针织辅料	zhēnzhīfǔliào	名	supplementary knitting materials	19
震荡	zhèndàng	动/名	shock	11
郑重	zhèngzhòng	形/副	serious, solemn	15
执意	zhíyì	动/副	insist on	16
指挥	zhǐhuī	动/名	command	13
指令	zhǐlìng	动/名	give instruction	12
置身于	zhìshēnyú	动	place oneself in	19
秩序	zhìxù	名	order, rules	16
制约	zhìyuē	动/名	constrain	16
忠诚	zhōngchéng	名	loyalty	11
中庸之道	zhōngyóngzhidào	名	Doctrine of the Mean (Confucian text)	11
主干	zhǔgàn	名	trunk, mainstay	11
主张	zhǔzhāng	动/名	advocate, proposal	11
转败为胜	zhuǎnbàiwéishèng	动	turn defeat into victory	13
拙劣	zhuōliè	形/副	poor, inferior	13
着力	zhuólì	副	forcefully	20
卓越	zhuóyuè	形	outstanding	11
咨询	zīxún	动/名	consult, consultancy	19
自动扶梯	zìdòngfútī	名	escalator	19
自身修养	zìshēnxiūyǎng	名	personal self improvement	12

自知之明	zìzhīzhīmíng	名	wisdom that comes from self knowledge	12
中国工商银行	Zhōngguógōngshāng yínháng	专名	Industrial and Commercial Bank of China	18
中国银行	Zhōngguóyínháng	专名	Bank of China	18
遵循	zūnxún	动	comply with; follow	12